The New Pentecostal Message?

The New Pentecostal Message?

— An Introduction to the Prosperity Movement —

LEWIS BROGDON

Foreword by Vinson Synan

CASCADE *Books* • Eugene, Oregon

THE NEW PENTECOSTAL MESSAGE?
An Introduction to the Prosperity Movement

Copyright © 2015 Lewis Brogdon. All rights reserved. Except for brief quotations in critical publications or reviews, no part of this book may be reproduced in any manner without prior written permission from the publisher. Write: Permissions, Wipf and Stock Publishers, 199 W. 8th Ave., Suite 3, Eugene, OR 97401.

Cascade Books
An Imprint of Wipf and Stock Publishers
199 W. 8th Ave., Suite 3
Eugene, OR 97401

www.wipfandstock.com

ISBN 13: 978-1-4982-0589-4

Cataloguing-in-Publication Data

Brogdon, Lewis.

The new Pentecostal message ? : an introduction to the prosperity movement / Lewis Brogdon.

xvi + 112 p. ; 23 cm. Includes bibliographical references.

ISBN 13: 978-1-4982-0589-4

1. African Americans—Religion. 2. Faith movement (Hagin) 3. Wealth—Religious aspects. I. Title.

BR563.N4 B675 2015
Manufactured in the U.S.A.   06/12/2015

Contents

Foreword by Vinson Synan | vii
Introduction | ix

CHAPTER 1
Changing the Way We Study the Prosperity Movement | 1

CHAPTER 2
Changing the Narrative of American Pentecostalism | 25

CHAPTER 3
Is Prosperity Teaching a New Heresy? | 46

CHAPTER 4
Is Prosperity Teaching Good News to the Poor? | 71

CHAPTER 5
Is Prosperity Teaching the New Pentecostal Message? | 90

APPENDIX: CRITIQUES OF PROSPERITY THEOLOGY | 103

Bibliography | 107

Foreword

SEVERAL YEARS AGO LEWIS Brogdon was a PhD student in my classes in the Regent University School of Divinity. I remember him as a very bright student who did good work and was very popular with other students. Early on he showed an interest in the prosperity movement among Pentecostals and conducted research that led to seminar papers in three of his courses. This book is an outgrowth of that research.

Growing up in Bluefield, Virginia in a Pentecostal Holiness church, in addition to spending years in a nondenominational church that emphasized a healthy version of the prosperity gospel, he writes as an insider with insights that can only be gained by one who experienced the movement firsthand. A chapter of the book details his years in the Redeeming Life Christian Center, pastored by the Bishop Fred Brown, a graduate of Rhema Bible Institute in Broken Arrow, Oklahoma, founded by Kenneth Hagin. He knows whereof he speaks. As an African-American scholar, he writes clearly about the effects of the prosperity gospel on the black church in America and also in the megachurches in Africa and those in the far-flung African diaspora. Here he sees both positive and negative results of the prosperity teaching in black Pentecostal churches.

In contrast to others, he sees the roots of the movement in the preaching of such healing evangelists as Oral Roberts and A. A. Allen, rather than in the faith movement led by Kenneth Hagin, who got his inspiration from E. W. Kenyon's metaphysical writings. Thus it was a Pentecostal phenomenon in the beginning with such Faith teachers as Hagin, Kenneth Copeland, and Fred Price, coming later under the influence of Roberts. Brogdon goes to great lengths to present all sides of the theological questions raised by the many critics of the movement such as Hank Hannegraff, Bruce Barron, Jeremiah Wright, Gordon Fee, D. R. McConnell, and John MacArthur. In contrast to these, he presents the pro-prosperity arguments of Fred Price, Kenneth Hagin, and John Avanzini, among others. In answer to the question "Is the prosperity gospel heretical?" he answers an emphatic "no," but he admits that there are hermeneutical and theological nuances that need correction.

In summary, he calls for a more balanced presentation of prosperity teachings. In the last chapter, Brogdon surveys the problem of the vast unequal distribution of wealth in the world, with the richest 1 percent owning as much as the poorest 90 percent of the world's population. This inequality, he points out, must be addressed by Pentecostals who are inspired by the prosperity gospel. He also asserts that they need to speak to such other intractable problems as racial injustice and the inherent problems of unfettered capitalism. In several places Brogdon has inserted tables with helpful quotations from writers on all sides of the debate over prosperity teachings. His bibliography, although not exhaustive, is very helpful for those who wish to learn more about the subject.

This book, *The New Pentecostal Message? An Introduction to the Prosperity Movement*, poses the question: is the prosperity gospel the "new Pentecostal message"? In answer, Brogdon fears that an overemphasis on material prosperity may come with the loss of the features that made Pentecostalism the fastest-growing religious movement on earth. If this results in a loss of teaching on the gifts of the Spirit and their being experienced in Pentecostal church life, then the prosperity gospel would be a great danger to the future of the movement. The solution offered by Brogdon is a balance that maintains the dynamics of traditional Pentecostal spirituality coupled with the hope of a better life on earth offered by the prosperity gospel. Brogdon's work is a valuable and thoughtful analysis of the movement that adds much to the literature on the prosperity gospel that has been produced thus far.

Vinson Synan
Dean Emeritus
Regent University School of Divinity

Introduction

THE PROSPERITY MOVEMENT HAS become a major tradition within the larger world of global Pentecostalism. There are a considerable number of churches and ministries that promote this brand of teaching in America and across the world. This movement's growth has been a subtheme within the larger narrative of Pentecostalism's explosive growth during the last two decades of the twentieth century and the first decade of the twenty-first century. As the Pentecostal message spread all over the world during this time, so did one of its most popular and controversial teachings. Pentecostal preachers promoted the message of Spirit-filled life, the importance of spiritual gifts, and the anointing, healing, and prosperity blessings that are made possible because of the atoning sacrifice of Jesus Christ and power of the Holy Spirit. But the story of the prosperity movement is rarely framed in this manner.

During the last two decades of the twentieth century, this movement exploded around the world. Religious scholars and church leaders became increasingly interested in this Pentecostal movement and wrote many books. These works have been too broad, mostly negative, sometimes inflammatory, and often condemnatory. Books such as D. R. McConnell's *A Different Gospel* became standard sources of authority on the movement that later scholars utilized in their evaluations of prosperity teaching. As a result, some of the later works on the prosperity movement seem to share common concerns, and in my opinion are based on three flawed assumptions. First, many assume that the prosperity movement is a Word of Faith movement and that Word of Faith teaching is a reformulated version of New Thought metaphysics and Mind Science. The second assumption is that the prosperity movement is solely a reflection of American capitalistic and cultural values. Some believe prosperity teaching reflects the American obsession with money and success. Third, some scholars and church leaders assume that prosperity teaching can only be justified by distorting biblical texts and supposedly orthodox and uniform Christian beliefs. These three assumptions, common in scholarly works, are rooted in a negative predisposition toward both the Word of Faith movement and the prosperity message. These assumptions preclude scholars and leaders from engaging in a deeper study of the prosperity movement's history and thought and diminish any possibility that the message may have constructive features for Pentecostal and broader ecumenical discourse.

These three assumptions also miss important issues that could change the tenor of how this popular teaching is studied, which could possibly advance our understanding of this movement and what it could teach us about contemporary religious movements. Regarding these assumptions I would say first that beliefs about prosperity predate the Word of Faith movement and are by no means a product of Pentecostalism. All Protestant traditions have beliefs about the benevolent and generous nature of God toward creation. Christians have taught that God blesses saints or the church for hundreds of years. This is not a new belief. Second, the belief that the prosperity movement is solely a reflection of American cultural beliefs is valid, but only to a certain extent. Prosperity teaching is influenced by American cultural values, but they are not the only influence. There are religious influences as well. There is no doubt that this movement is influenced by American cultural values, especially those informed by capitalistic beliefs, but all traditions in American Christianity are influenced positively and negatively by its cultural norms and mores. The deeper and more complex issue is the extent of influence, but that is difficult, if not impossible, to ascertain. It is also important that those who critique this movement acknowledge the baggage of their church traditions, past and present, on this same issue. There is not a single tradition of the church with a perfect track record on the issue of money and its intersection with faith and ministry. This line of reasoning also undercuts having to do any study on Pentecostal theological beliefs that inform the prosperity message. In fact, the failure of many works to situate this movement with Pentecostalism is a glaring oversight and grave error. Lastly, the critique that the movement's beliefs are possible only when Scripture is distorted is an overstatement because it ignores the preponderance of passages of Scripture that speak of God's desire to bless or prosper creation and his covenant people. Also, the belief that prosperity teaching contradicts orthodox teaching is simplistic.

— Introduction — xi

Orthodoxy has always been in the eye of the beholder. Christians do not share a uniform belief system about anything. and even contest Christian identity.

These radically critical works, though well intended, have misunderstood aspects of this movement and misrepresented the movement to the broader religious community in different ways. In doing this, they have done a disservice to our understanding of it and the people who are a part of its churches and ministries. It is not fair to evaluate a movement if it is not given a historically accurate and theologically balanced presentation at the table of theological discourse. It is time to move beyond the caricature of the prosperity pimp or money preacher to serious contextual analysis of the movement. I fear that more scholars and popular religious leaders will continue to produce writings and make public statements that are uncritical, inflammatory, and in the end do not help us to recognize the diversity of this religious movement and the debate about it within Pentecostalism and Protestantism. I hope that what follows is an attempt to trace the historical development of this movement, to recognize the diversity this movement takes within Pentecostalism, and to take seriously its theological beliefs, which are rooted in the Bible, Christian theological beliefs, and distinct Pentecostal teachings.

A MOVEMENT THAT COMMANDS ATTENTION

The widespread influence of Pentecostalism and the popularity of this brand of teaching command continuing and critical scholarly attention. There is a pervasive belief that the economic collapse of 2008 effectively ended the prosperity movement in America. I fear that as a consequence of this belief, scholars will continue to ignore this movement as an object of study. Even if the popularity of the movement has faded or is less prominent, it is still important to study. Let me provide two reasons. First, if we do not have a better understanding of this movement's history within Pentecostalism, we may not discern the ways the movement may morph in response to a new economic climate. If, as I will argue, the movement emerged within Pentecostalism and then throughout neo-Charismatic nondenominational churches around the world, then it means this message has been morphing for decades and we need a historical narrative that helps us to understand it. The worst thing we can do is to have a narrow or distorted history of this movement or, worse yet, continue with the "money preacher" caricature. If we continue to do this, we will be oblivious to what's next. I believe this movement will and has already begun to morph. This takes me to my second reason. The worst thing we can do is to ignore prosperity teaching churches. Close and careful attention should be paid to these churches and the future of this movement and message. Who is paying attention to what they are preaching now? What adjustments have they made to their message? How have they responded to three decades of critiques? What aspects of prosperity teaching have infiltrated non-Pentecostal churches and how is it impacting their congregations and preaching? Not only is no one answering these questions, I fear no one is even asking them. This movement commands attention especially when one considers the potential influence this movement has on shaping global Pentecostal spirituality and theology, a question I will take up in the final chapter of this book.

The prosperity movement also raises deeper questions that all Christian traditions and justice-minded leaders should critically explore. The movement raises theological questions about our understanding and beliefs about divine blessings and God's care for creation and God's covenant people. How do we articulate beliefs about God's care for his creatures? Or does God not care about the spiritual and material needs of people? The prosperity movement raises hermeneutical questions about the uses of Scripture to require, inspire, and regulate financial giving to churches, ministries, and pastors. How are we to interpret commands about tithing and giving? Do we accept the belief that God curses people who do not tithe? The prosperity movement raises ethical questions. Is it ethical to receive or take financial gifts from marginalized persons or groups? Is it ethical to require marginalized persons or groups to give to churches? Is this another form of injustice layered on top of existing injustices linked to slavery and systemic racism that created large disparities and inequities? The prosperity movement raises pragmatic questions for pastors and other religious leaders. How do you generate revenue to do ministry so you can do good in the community and the world? Congregations need money to operate and they can only do ministry to the extent that concerned members give toward ministry endeavors. These very difficult and complex issues intersect with the prosperity movement in a number of ways.

Prosperity teachers have beliefs about God's care for people. They use the Bible to talk about God's care and what Christians are supposed to do to experience this kind of care. And they expect people to give money to ministries as a way to experience divine blessings and to support the work of ministry. To a certain extent these teachers and their churches are doing the exact same thing others are doing. The only difference is the justification for doing it and maybe the level of extravagance of the advocates. Critics are quick to point out that some prosperity teachers own jets and drive expensive cars. Critics are quick to point this out. But mainline and Catholic churches have their own forms of extravagance. They have a plethora of wealthy institutions and organizations with millions of dollars in endowments, some of which are connected to centuries of slavery and exploitative labor practices from the industrial age. The presidents and high-level officers of these organizations live extravagant lives, too. They fly first class. They own expensive homes, sometimes in other countries. They take expensive vacations. The difference is that they get the privilege of using institutional and organizational dollars and claim that their work is for the maintenance and development of the institution. Oh, and they do not call themselves prosperity teachers. What I am trying to argue is that these issues intersect with all Christian traditions. There are both points of comparison and contrast of this movement with other traditions, and the study of this movement ought to be framed with this recognition.

BOOK SUMMARY

The first chapter will examine the history of the movement. This chapter will begin with a discussion of the numerical growth of the movement in the eighties and nineties, its national and global prominence that is attested to by large ministries, national news coverage, and multiple studies of the movement. I will also take up the issue of the origin of the prosperity movement and present my argument that I believe many scholarly studies operate with a mistaken theory of the origins of the movement. Afterwards, I will provide a historical survey of the development, growth, and beliefs of key advocates of prosperity, focusing particularly on two healing evangelists of the fifties and sixties: Oral Roberts and A. A. Allen. In addition, I will discuss the growth of the movement because of the Word of Faith movement's increasing emphasis on prosperity in the late seventies, especially throughout the eighties, and on into the late twentieth and early twenty-first centuries, in which hybrid or neoprosperity churches exploded onto the global Pentecostal scene.

Chapter 2 will explore the history of the prosperity movement by giving attention to its origins within Pentecostalism. In particular, I examine how the prosperity movement symbolized a changing narrative of Pentecostalism. American Pentecostals are no longer considered tongue-talking holy rollers, but have become more aligned with mainstream church tradition. This growing acceptance of Pentecostalism, along with the increasing prominence of the prosperity doctrine, divided Pentecostals and created tensions about whether the narrative of success and prosperity should characterize people of the Spirit. There is a heated debate among Pentecostals about money and the shift in emphasis that began to take place during the time under study in this chapter. This narrative will form the backdrop of my study of the theology of the movement. Prosperity theology must first be examined within the broader context of Pentecostalism and be viewed as an internal debate between Pentecostals. After this, one can move on to study distinct streams of thought like those in the Word of Faith movement. Too many studies begin there and miss the broader context of Pentecostalism.

Chapter 3 will show that beginning in the late 1980s and extending into 2007, this burgeoning movement was increasingly subjected to critique regarding its approach to biblical interpretation and the pervasive influence of non-Christian ideologies and beliefs. These are some of the reasons scholars and popular pastors charge this movement with being heretical and cult-like. The chapter will survey major arguments against the prosperity movement beginning in the eighties and extending to contemporary works. Ideally this chapter should help both to delineate and systematize issues germane to the theology of the movement. The last section will document the explosive debates that are erupting around the movement among black religious scholars who feel this message does more harm than good. Then in chapter 4, I will delve into the appeal of this movement among the poor and marginalized by asking, "Is prosperity teaching good news to the poor?" The prosperity movement has many theological problems and inconsistencies to work through in the coming years, but there are strands of it that do good, especially for poor and marginalized people, and do not always fit popular critiques of prosperity teaching or teachers. I also believe it is important to give some account of the deeper reasons people find this message to be meaningful and life-giving. So in this chapter, I will investigate why I believe people from marginalized communities and church traditions find the movement and its teachings so appealing. Given the tendency of most scholarly studies to focus on popular televangelists in large urban cities and my desire to change the way we study this movement, I will turn to a small prosperity-teaching congregation in southern West Virginia and provide an ethnographic and theological study of this movement that shows the promise this teaching holds for the poor. This methodological move has the potential to take the study of this movement in new directions.

The final chapter will provide a culminating look at the prosperity movement and the future of Pentecostalism. My question is, "does the prosperity movement represent the future of global Pentecostalism?" Success has possibly become the new central tenet of American Pentecostalism. A large part of this chapter will discuss the concerns I have about prosperity gospel becoming the new Pentecostal message. There are reasons I believe this could hurt both American and global Pentecostalism, as well as reasons, if the prosperity movement undergoes change, this could revitalize it. Pentecostals will have a decision to make in the coming years.

— CHAPTER 1 —

Changing the Way We Study the Prosperity Movement

THE PROSPERITY MOVEMENT BECAME one of the dominant features of global Pentecostalism in the last two decades of the twentieth century and the first decade of the twenty-first century. In recent years, it is becoming one of the most significant developments in American Protestantism. Prosperity preaching has significantly affected how people think about money, faith, and the church both in America and globally. This is probably because some of the largest churches in America preach varying forms of prosperity teaching. Joel Osteen, the widely popular pastor of the 30,000-member Lakewood Church in Houston, is one such example. Kenneth Hagin Jr. in Oklahoma, Mark Chirona in Florida, I. V. Hillard in Houston, and Michael Freeman in Baltimore all pastor large congregations. Prosperity teaching has become popular even in smaller cities and towns. For example, Leroy Thompson in Darrow, Louisiana is a major proponent of prosperity teaching. What do these pastors and churches have in common besides thousands of members in their churches? They preach prosperity and they do it in a culture where there is widespread appeal for this form of teaching.

Nothing captures the prominence of the prosperity movement in America today quite like a feature in *Time* magazine. Its treatment in the September 18, 2006 edition, headlined "Does God Want You To Be Rich?" is one indicator of the prominence and widespread influence of this movement. According to the article, 61 percent of Christians polled agreed that God wants people to be financially prosperous while 26 percent disagreed. 49 percent of the Christians polled disagreed that poverty can be a blessing from God and 44 percent did not agree with the principle of following the example of Jesus by being poor.[1] This movement seems to resonate with millions of Americans and is possibly one reason for its success and popularity in the nineties and the first decade of the twenty-first century.

The prosperity phenomenon is not just an American religious movement, but a global one. Prosperity teaching churches are growing in Africa, Asia, and South America. For example, David Oyedepo pastors Canaanland Church in Lagos, Nigeria, a 55,000-plus-member prosperity church. David Yonggi Cho pastors Full Gospel Church in Seoul, South Korea, that preaches prosperity to over 800,000 members. Some critics of the movement thought that it was strictly an American phenomenon that would not flourish in poor countries. That belief has proven to be false. According to a recent report by the Pew Forum on Religion and Public Life, prosperity churches are the fastest growing churches in Africa, including one-fourth of Nigeria's population, more than one-third of South Africa's, and 56 percent of Kenya's population.[2] When asked if God granted material prosperity to believers with faith, 85 percent of Kenyan Pentecostals, 90 percent of South African Pentecostals, and 95 percent of Nigerian Pentecostals responded yes.[3] Such startling data reinforces not only the prominence of the movement but the importance of the intersection between faith and economic realities for many Pentecostal Christians. The assumption for many African Pentecostals is that God cares about their economic condition. But there is by no means unanimity about the movement's importance in Africa, a continent facing significant economic challenges for millions of people.

The sheer magnitude of these churches both in America and the rest of the world is influencing a growing segment of the Christian world. As a result of the tremendous growth of this movement, more public and scholarly attention is being given to its history and theology and their implications for the broader church for the past two decades. The spring edition of the *African American Pulpit* addressed trends in the black church. The prosperity movement was mentioned as a major trend in many black

1. Biema and Chu, "Does God Want You to be Rich?," 56.

2. 2006 Pew Forum on Religion and Public Life, quoted in Phiri and Maxwell, "Gospel Riches," 23–24.

3. Ibid.

— Changing the Way We Study the Prosperity Movement — 3

churches.[4] In May 2007, Anderson Cooper's nightly news program *360* ended with a documentary piece on contemporary Christian issues with a discussion of the prosperity phenomenon. ABC News did a story on the movement on January 23, 2008, after a United States senator sent a letter to six prosperity teachers questioning their lavish lifestyles and whether these ministries are abusing their tax-exempt status as nonprofit organizations.[5] Lectures given by Howard University ethicist Cheryl Sanders at the 2007 Hampton Minister's Conference interrogated this movement's popularity in the African American community. This is one of the largest black church gatherings in the country. After one of Sanders's lectures, the worship leader led an altar call giving people the opportunity to repent for preaching the prosperity gospel. Robert Franklin's new book *Crisis in the Village* contends that this movement poses the greatest threat to the black community.[6] The highly acclaimed magazine *Gospel Today* took up the prosperity debate in its May-June 2007 issue. One of the most prominent gatherings of highly educated African American clergy is the Samuel Dewitt Proctor Conference. In 2005 the conference was held in Atlanta and discussed the growing influence of the prosperity movement in America. Again, speakers were interested in how popular the movement had become in the black community and black churches. What is clear from the increased attention is the negativity of the coverage and assessment of the movement. Attention was given to excesses and abuses caused by and linked to this message, as if that is all there is to the movement. This leads me to a very important point that I began with in the introduction but will now discuss further, which is to explore how this movement is studied or approached by scholars.

HOW THE PROSPERITY MOVEMENT IS STUDIED

For the past two-plus decades, religious scholars have been studying the origins of the movement, its teachings, and how best to respond to its tremendous growth. This increased attention and popular media coverage has led to a fierce debate about the orthodoxy of these teachings and the meaning of this movement in a capitalistic and consumerist society. Some religious scholars and church leaders believe that the movement

---

4. Simmons, "Trends in the African American Church," 9–16.
5. Tuchman, "What is a Christian?"
6. Franklin, *Crisis in the Village*.

is heretical. And those who may not lay the charge of heresy question the theology and hermeneutical principles employed to support these teachings. Some go so far as to claim that the movement is a product of a capitalist and consumerist society and not one with theological beliefs rooted in a particular Christian tradition. The perennial questions revolve around the basic teachings and historical origins of the movement.

What I have discovered is that popular works on the prosperity movement have given a thorough analysis of the non-Christian origins of this form of teaching. Most scholarly and popular studies of the movement argue that prosperity teaching is based on New Thought metaphysics and Mind Science. They assert that Word of Faith teachers such as Ken Hagin Sr., Fred Price, Ken and Gloria Copeland, and Creflo Dollar take non-Christian beliefs and use the Bible to sanction a system of belief that is erroneous and possibly heretical. However, these works have not examined the movement's history within the classical Pentecostal and Charismatic movement from the 1950s to the present. There is an exception: the recently published book *Blessed: The History of the Prosperity Movement*, by Duke University historian Kate Bowler.[7] The lack of analysis about the movement's origins within Pentecostalism is a problem. It leads to inaccuracies about the history and theology of the movement.

I want to amend on some points and correct on other points by writing a history that views this movement as ultimately a Pentecostal one. I also hope that this history will complement important studies on the movement currently in print like D. R. McConnell's *A Different Gospel* (1995), Andrew Perriman's *Faith, Health, and Prosperity* (2003), Bruce Barron's *The Health and Wealth Gospel* (1987), Robert Bowman's *The Word of Faith Controversy* (2001), Milmon F. Harrison's *Righteous Riches* (2007), Debra Mumford's *Exploring Prosperity Preaching* (2012), and the recent comprehensive study by Kate Bowler, *Blessed* (2013). I also hope to advance the study of this movement and encourage continued scholarly interest in why this movement has struck a chord in the religious imagination of millions of people globally and why it has become one of the popular features of global Pentecostalism.

The first step in advancing the study of this movement is to critique and interrogate the dominant posture toward its teaching, which is largely negative and at times inaccurate. I have wonder, "Why would one study a movement without an adequate understanding of the historical

---

7. Bowler, *Blessed*.

and ideological context out of which the movement emerged?" Too many critics do so because they do not take Pentecostalism seriously as a subject of scholarly inquiry. It is too common for scholarly studies to launch critiques about the prosperity movement without a basic understanding of the history of Pentecostalism, the basic features of Pentecostal theologies, or an awareness of how a failure to understand Pentecostalism discredits attempts to examine one of its popular movements. While I am not attempting to silence those who are critical of the movement, because I am very critical of many aspects, it is my aim to advance the study of prosperity teaching beyond just critiques to an overall understanding of the history and thought of the movement within the world of Pentecostalism. Scholars of religion need research on the history and thought of the prosperity movement as it evolved from within the complex world of American Pentecostalism. And this is where most works on the prosperity movement fall short. These works do not account for the vast diversity within global Pentecostalism and I am not sure if these scholars know where the Word of Faith movement fits within the larger matrix of global Pentecostalism.

The second step in advancing the study of this movement is for mainline scholars to get over its growth and popularity. The tremendous growth of the prosperity movement in the eighties, nineties, and the first decade of the twenty-first century has been an overriding foci and preoccupation by religious scholars. For them, "everybody is on the prosperity bandwagon" or "prosperity is the new and only message for megachurches." Prosperity teaching becomes a scapegoat or a straw man for megachurches, nondenominational churches, or growing churches. "They must be growing because they are preaching prosperity" is a common critique heard at conferences and on panels. After all, anything popular or growing has to be wrong. There is so much more to the prosperity movement than its growth and popularity. Numerical growth and decline does not tell us everything about a popular religious movement. However, this common scholarly tendency needs to be interrogated.

I suspect that some of the interest in the movement's growth is fueled by denominational jealousy and rivalry from those in traditions experiencing significant numerical decline. In other words, ecclesial self-interest is very much a part of the concern in this movement. Mainline scholars who are so critical of the prosperity movement are not entirely honest about their motives. The same can be said for evangelical critics. Their preoccupation with this "growing" movement and all that is wrong with it has betrayed an appropriate lack of hindsight on their part and a clear bias against Pentecostalism. Some scholars have given no attention to the fact that prosperity movements are a part of all Christian traditions and they have ignored their own tradition's history of economic exploitation during slavery and reconstruction. They have also failed to launch an adequate critique of their own tradition's form of the prosperity gospel and its consumption of capitalistic greed as it built large Main Street churches, universities, colleges, and seminaries with endowments in the millions. With dwindling mainline numbers and influence, now these scholars are interested in economic justice and exploitation by pastors in other denominations. That is why I believe the tenor of study needs to change.

For this and other reasons, I believe it is time to change the way we study the prosperity movement. It is time to go beyond the overly negative and sometimes uncritical rhetoric about the movement that is prominent in scholarly writings and mainline church circles to an analysis that is marked by three things: (1) an approach that takes Pentecostalism seriously, (2) an approach that is more forthright about their church's respective histories on the subject of economic justice and its own theology of blessing or prosperity, and (3) an approach that recognizes the theological complexity required when discussing and thinking theologically about the intersections of money, faith, congregations, preaching, and ministry. This study seeks to do this kind of work.

THE MISTAKEN ORIGINS THESIS

Another step is to interrogate the popular theory about the origins of the prosperity movement. When studying the history of the prosperity movement one must inevitably begin with the contentious origins debate. Popular evangelical works like Hank Hannegraff's *Christianity in Crisis* argue that prosperity teaching is a reformulated form of New Thought metaphysics and Christian Science and that these teachings have no basis in the teachings of Scripture.[8] They do so largely because of the work of D. R. McConnell in the book *A Different Gospel*. McConnell, a charismatic, argues that the Word of Faith movement should not be considered a part of the charismatic movement, but actually owes its roots to E. W. Kenyon and nineteenth-century metaphysical cults. McConnell bases his

---

8. Hannegraff, *Christianity in Crisis*.

conclusion on two factors: Kenyon's affinity for metaphysical teaching and Ken Hagin's plagiarism of Kenyon.[9] As a result of this, he concludes that Word of Faith teaching is actually more akin to metaphysical thought than Christian beliefs rooted in Scripture. In other words, he, like many others who follow his line of reasoning, believes that the movement is heretical at its core.

In fact, critiques of the prosperity movement are often directed against the Word of Faith context and the framework established by McConnell's *A Different Gospel*. I believe this approach has three weaknesses. First, it is based on a flawed assumption that all of Kenyon's teachings were derived from metaphysical thought. Second, it treats prosperity teaching solely as a product of the Word of Faith movement and discounts other influences like Pentecostal thought. This assumption fails to recognize that prosperity teaching predated the advent of the Word of Faith movement. Third, it fails to account for the voices and traditions that support various facets of prosperity thinking in the American secular arena, earlier Protestant traditions, and African American religious traditions. While it is important to account for influences like New Thought metaphysics and Christian Science, one does not necessarily need to follow McConnell's flawed approach. I am not alone in this line of thinking.

In Robert Bowman's book *The Word Faith Controversy*, he exposes some of the deficiencies of McConnell's argument both as it relates to other influences on Kenyon's teaching and the roots of the Word of Faith movement.[10] Bowman argues that the roots of the Word of Faith movement are in the evangelical Faith Cure M\movement as well as Pentecostal healing evangelists like William Branham and Oral Roberts, not explicitly nineteenth-century metaphysical New Thought. And he challenges McConnell's work on the movement for mistaking Kenyon as a cultic metaphysical teacher by demonstrating that his use of Kenyon quotes did not provide accurate depictions of his teaching. Bowman argues that Kenyon rejected New Thought cults and demonstrated his repudiation of such teachings by only ministering in strictly Baptist and Pentecostal churches.

---

9. McConnell chronicles how Ken Hagin plagiarized the writings of E. W. Kenyon and therefore concludes that the real founder of Word of Faith teaching is Kenyon and not Hagin. This work is one of the more important works on Hagin and the movement, especially because it seriously questions if these teachings were received by direct revelation. See McConnell, *A Different Gospel*.

10. Bowman, *The Word of Faith Controversy*, 86.

In order to get a better grasp of the Word of Faith movement one should also understand its origins in the classical Pentecostal tradition through two prominent healing evangelists, A. A. Allen and Oral Roberts, before moving to Ken Hagin and assessing his link to Kenyon. One should not begin with Hagin and the metaphysical connection as if classical Pentecostals were not already hearing earlier forms of prosperity teaching during the healing revivals of the fifties and sixties, a movement that laid the groundwork for the charismatic renewal in mainline churches. Once Hagin is historically situated in the Pentecostal healing tradition, his teachings can be analyzed in light of the Pentecostal framework and his apparent plagiarism of Kenyon. Then one can trace prominent prosperity teachers who were influenced by this founding figure of the Word of Faith movement. Hagin was instrumental in the development of an altogether different strand of teaching but his framework was very much informed by classical Pentecostalism, in addition to the undeniable influence of Kenyon. Too many contemporary works portray Hagin as one who was not influenced by the theology of Pentecostals. To them he relied on Kenyon only. Instead, I would argue that both were important influences. For example, his beliefs in the baptism of the Spirit, prayer, healing, and God's immanence are definitely influenced by Pentecostalism.[11] And these beliefs influence his views on prosperity. For example, Hagin taught that the blessings of healing and prosperity are for believers who have been filled with the Holy Spirit and walk in the Spirit. The experience with the Spirit is requisite for believers to flow in the gifts of the Spirit, such as faith. Now this insistence and expectation that one is filled with the Holy Spirit is not a belief from New Thought metaphysics or Mind Science. Hagin did not get this belief from Kenyon either. He was introduced and formed in the Assemblies of God, a Pentecostal church tradition that teaches the need for salvation and Spirit baptism.

THE PROSPERITY MOVEMENT AS A PENTECOSTAL MOVEMENT

Without a better understanding of the historical framework out of which the prosperity movement emerged, one may be led to believe that this movement suddenly emerged from a leader who Christianized secular

---

11. See Hagin, *Bible Prayer Study Course*; *Bible Faith Study Course*; and *The Holy Spirit and His Gifts*.

or non-Christian ideas beginning in the seventies, or that it is something new in American religion. When the movement is solely viewed as a Word of Faith movement, one misses developments and ideas from Pentecostalism that are important antecedents to the Word of Faith and prosperity movements. There are three viable reasons for situating the prosperity movement in the broader context of Pentecostalism.

First, Word of Faith teachers were not the first Christian leaders to teach some form of prosperity. Earlier forms of a kind of prosperity teaching sided with the Roman Empire, built St. Peter's Cathedral, and justified slavery and industrialization. Vinson Synan mentions this in his newly published work entitled *An Eyewitness Remembers*. The Protestant work ethic is an earlier and different form of prosperity teaching used to justify capitalism and exploitation. It maintained that if people worked hard and lived a virtuous life they would experience God's blessings because America was believed to be a "city on a hill." Rich "robber barons" like Cornelius Vanderbilt, John D. Rockefeller, Andrew Carnegie, James Duke, and J. P. Morgan—mainly Baptists, Presbyterians, Congregationalists, Methodists, and Episcopalians—built churches and hired preachers who justified their privilege. The historic Riverside Church in New York City was built with Rockefeller money. Russell Conwell, a Baptist and founder of Temple University, published a book entitled *Acres of Diamonds*.[12] Prosperity teachings run deep in the Christian tradition. Pentecostalism is just the newest tradition to take it up in such a concentrated manner.

Second, Pentecostals advocated prosperity teaching before the Word of Faith movement came onto the scene. Ministers like Thomas Wyatt in the thirties and A. A. Allen, Gordon Lindsay, and Oral Roberts in the fifties and sixties all taught a form of prosperity. The Pentecostal healing revivals of the fifties and sixties were an essential precursor to both Charismatic renewal within the Catholic Church and Protestant denominations, and more importantly the proliferation of independent nondenominational neo-Charismatic churches and ministries, which paved the way for the Word of Faith movement.

Third, Oral Roberts's seed faith principle, his revelation concerning 3 John 2, and the resultant conviction that God is good were essential developments in the larger Pentecostal tradition that find fuller expressions in Word of Faith teachings. Oral Roberts is an important figure

---

12. For all these developments, see Synan, *An Eyewitness Remembers the Century of the Holy Spirit*, 113–26.

in the evolution of prosperity teaching. More than anyone else, Roberts was responsible for introducing Pentecostal spirituality and beliefs to the wider American religious audience through the mediums of television, radio, and healing crusades. He was the first to begin building a large religious empire without denominational support and so introduced the "hyperfundraising" practice into the tradition. The big business of ministry in the nondenominational sector can reasonably be attributed to him. Roberts represents one of the first Pentecostals of the mid-to-late twentieth century to bridge both the Pentecostal and non-Charismatic world. Roberts is the key to understanding the later emergence of prosperity theology.

I first learned about the important link between Oral Roberts and Ken Hagin in an interview with the Pentecostal Charismatic historian Vinson Synan. Synan's father served as a bishop in the Pentecostal Holiness Church, where Roberts's parents were both ordained ministers. Also, Roberts was a pastor in the Pentecostal Holiness Church and worked closely with many leaders Synan knows personally. He maintains that Oral Roberts was a major influence on Kenneth Hagin and it was widely known in Pentecostal circles that Oral Roberts was the one who influenced Hagin. For Synan, the common thread was not necessarily Kenyon, but Napoleon Hill's influential book *Think and Grow Rich*. Oral Roberts was heavily influenced by this book and promoted it in the sixties. This form of New Thought metaphysics teaches that one should think of and visualize success in order for it to be realized. This information challenges the Kenyon and Hagin narrative that dominates the literature about the movement.[13]

One could argue that Oral Roberts is a founding figure of both the Word of Faith movement and prosperity teaching, even though Ken Hagin Sr. centralized and popularized prosperity teaching in a way that Roberts did not. Roberts's emphasis was healing and the overall expansion of his ministry both on television and later with a hospital and university. He used seed faith principles to facilitate fund-raising efforts toward these larger endeavors, whereas Hagin focused on faith, healing, and prosperity, making them the central tenets of a new form of teaching that he often called the Word of Faith. Hagin used the Rhema Ministerial Association, the Rhema Training Center, and annual conferences to promote these teachings nationally and internationally. He also influenced

---

13. Synan, interview at Regent University, October 11, 2006.

three pastor-teachers of the eighties who would go on to influence millions of people with these teachings: Kenneth Copeland, Fred Price, and Hagin's son Ken Hagin Jr.

THE TERM *PROSPERITY*

When studying this movement, two problems emerge. First, the term *prosperity* is misunderstood and too vague. Gordon Fee describes it as the gospel of wealth.[14] He and many other critics think that prosperity teaching is exclusively the belief that God wants Christians to be rich. While some advocates of prosperity teaching may say this, their understanding of prosperity goes far beyond just being rich. The term prosperity and its meaning is a complex matter reflecting the influence of Pentecostal beliefs, secular beliefs, and religious beliefs that fall outside Christian teaching. Related to the misunderstanding of the term, a second problem is the failure to discern the various strands of prosperity teaching within the broader global Pentecostal movement. Because scholars define the movement through the narrow lens of "God wants Christians to be rich," they ignore or minimize the diverse ways prosperity themes are preached in Pentecostal, Charismatic, and nondenominational or neo-Charismatic churches and ministries.

In my study of the prosperity movement, I discovered at least eight distinct emphases or types of prosperity teaching within the various strands of global Pentecostalism. Below is a sample of prosperity teachers and their beliefs about prosperity.

Table 1: Different Types of Prosperity Emphases within Pentecostalism

Seed Faith Prosperity—Teachers such as Oral Roberts, Ken Hagin Sr., Ken Hagin Jr., Fred Price, and Kenneth and Gloria Copeland claim that the key to prosperity is to utilize one's finances as seeds that can yield a harvest. They teach believers to give money to good ministries that are viewed as "good ground" and to expect to receive a harvest.

Positive Confession Prosperity—Teachers such as Ken Hagin Sr., Ken Hagin Jr., Fred Price, Kenneth and Gloria Copeland, and Creflo Dollar instruct believers that the key to prosperity is the positive confession of faith. One can confess their way to a healthy and wealthy life. One can name it and claim it.

---

14. Fee, *The Disease of Health and Wealth Gospels*.

Prosperity as Debt Management—Teachers like Fred Price and Creflo Dollar claim that prosperity is attained when believers learn to manage credit and eliminate debt using faith and wisdom.

Supernatural Prosperity—Teachers such as John Avanzini and Leroy Thompson emphasize a miraculous dimension to prosperity when they interpret Malachi 3:10, Luke 6:38, and Ephesians 1:3. For them, God sends prosperity from heavenly storehouses and blessings are poured out of windows in heaven to believers. In the words of Leroy Thompson, "money cometh."

Prosperity as Empowerment—Teachers such as Ken Hagin Sr., Creflo Dollar, and Jerry Savelle teach that prosperity is a form of spiritual empowerment. Dollar refers to this as total life prosperity while Savelle refers to this as the prosperity of the soul. This brand of prosperity states that when believers receive and walk in the Spirit's power, they are able to manage all of life's challenges, including finances. They can walk in victory.

Prosperity as a Financial Breakthrough—African American Pentecostalism, such as the churches in the Virginia Third Ecclesiastical Jurisdiction, Church of God in Christ, teach a form of prosperity where God makes a way for the saints who are in need of financial help, a blessing or a breakthrough.

Prosperity as Divine Favor—Popular non-Word of Faith teachers like Joel Osteen and T. D. Jakes are proponents of the belief that God gives unearned favor like promotions, houses, cars, and ministry opportunities to those doing the divine will. This popular belief maintains that one's prosperity or blessing is based on God's grace and not one's educational background, work experience, race, gender or credit score.

Principled-Pragmatic Prosperity—Teachers such as Kenneth Copeland, Fred Price, T. D. Jakes, Creflo Dollar, I. V. Hilliard, and Michael Freeman advocate a pragmatic brand of this teaching. God blesses those who are in a covenant relationship with God, who work hard, who make smart decisions, and who live by both spiritual and worldly principles.

These variations in prosperity teaching help capture the breadth of the term and the movement within global Pentecostalism. This typology also demonstrates how teachers can advocate multiple strands of prosperity. Furthermore, it provides critics of the movement with strands that are worth more criticism than others. For example, the belief in supernatural prosperity that claims that God is going to cause money to come out of nowhere is worthy of criticism. On the other hand, how can one critique poor and marginalized persons who are looking to God and the church because they need a financial breakthrough to meet needs like food and heating bills? This mechanism also possibly accounts for why hybrid forms have been created that infiltrate and grow in non-Pentecostal traditions. I have heard type six and seven (Prosperity as Financial

Breakthrough and Prosperity as Divine Favor) preached in many African American Baptist churches in Virginia and Kentucky.

Beliefs about prosperity are broad and far more pervasive than a simplistic belief that God wants people to be rich. Such a distillation is almost absurd because it discounts different social influences, the matrix of religious beliefs, and variant expressions these beliefs take depending on cultural location. Let me provide further examples of this. First, in my years in the Church of God in Christ in Virginia, an African American Trinitarian Pentecostal denomination, we believed in prosperity but our understanding was qualitatively different than the Word of Faith brand. Prosperity for us was getting financial breakthroughs to meet our needs. We often criticized Word of Faith teachings because we thought its claims about healing and prosperity were not biblically sound or realistic. Second, T. D. Jakes is often labeled a prosperity preacher, but his teachings are different than Word of Faith teachers like Creflo Dollar and Fred Price. Jakes often talks about his roots and being poor growing up in the mountains of West Virginia, one of the poorest states in the country. Publications like *Can You Stand to be Blessed*[15] or *Maximize the Moment*[16] hardly fit the "name it and claim it" or "blab it and grab it" caricature prominent in mainline scholarly circles. Jakes inspires others to transcend obstacles like poverty through faith in God's power and plan for your life, and more importantly by drawing upon the gifts God has given every person. According to Jakes, this is the path that leads to success. After all, it worked for him.

To better understand and evaluate the prosperity movement, we have to understand the complex nature of the term *prosperity*. We must shift the study of this movement away from the belief that it is solely a product of the Word of Faith movement, a belief that dominates the literature. Instead, the prosperity movement should be studied as something that emerged from within global Pentecostalism, which has many differing churches and theological beliefs. It is not easy to classify the beliefs of millions of people. My study is only looking at the prosperity movement in America. A study of the prosperity movement in the global context would require a second volume.

The first thing to do is to introduce and discuss what I mean by the term *global Pentecostalism*. There were approximately 523 million

---

15. Jakes, *Can You Stand To Be Blessed?*
16. Jakes, *Maximize the Moment.*

Pentecostals in the world in 2000.[17] That figure has grown. Historians and scholars of Pentecostalism divide the movement into three major streams. The three streams consist of what historians and scholars call classical Pentecostalism, neo-Pentecostals or Charismatics, and neo-Charismatics or nondenominational "Spirit-filled" churches. Stan Burgess, in what is an important reference in the study of modern Pentecostalism, the *New International Dictionary of Pentecostal and Charismatic Movements,* classifies the movements accordingly: classical Pentecostalism, Charismatic renewal, and neo-Charismatic or third wave.[18] Classical Pentecostalism is a reference to North American Pentecostalism that originated in the early 1900s under the influence of Parham and Seymour. At Azusa from 1906 to 1909, the movement began and quickly became a major force, though it was persecuted and ridiculed for its emphasis on ecstatic gifts and its missionary zeal rooted in the belief that the end times were upon us. Out of this outpouring of spirituality, revivalism, evangelism, and mission activity, denominations were formed that either began in the Holiness movement, like the Church of God (Cleveland, Tennessee) and the Church of God in Christ, or after the Azusa Street Revival, like the Assemblies of God, Foursquare Church, and Pentecostal Assemblies of the World. Classical Pentecostals emphasize the doctrine of the baptism of the Holy Spirit with the evidence of speaking in tongues. For decades this was the distinguishing doctrine of the movement.

The Charismatic renewal movement began in the sixties and is characterized as a renewal movement within an existing denomination or tradition. In America there was an initial rejection of Pentecostal beliefs about tongues and the gifts of the Spirit. Pentecostals were mocked and scorned for decades by Catholic and Protestants. Eventually groups of people and sometimes entire congregations within these churches began experiencing the works of the Spirit and renewal emerged. While the gifts of the Spirit were accepted in these traditions, the doctrine of Spirit baptism with its evidential insistence on tongues was rejected. In the Charismatic movement the focus on tongues was replaced by a broader emphasis on the gifts and work of the Spirit. Catholicism was most influenced by Charismatic renewal and continues to represent a major influence in the movement. One of the distinguishing traits of the Charismatic movement was that Pentecostal beliefs about the Spirit

---

17. Burgess, ed., *New International Dictionary of the Pentecostal Charismatic Movement,* 282–84.

18. Ibid., xvii–xxi.

and second coming were adopted by Catholics and Protestants without renouncing their existing beliefs and practices. Charismatics merely added these beliefs and practices and remained in their traditions and denominations.

Finally, neo-Charismatics or the third wave represents quite a few different groups. Through the work of Allan Anderson, African indigenous groups challenged traditional conceptions of Pentecostal-like groups.[19] These groups emphasized the Spirit but were not connected to the Pentecostal or Charismatic movements. Therefore, third wavers or neo-Charismatics consist of indigenous groups that emphasize the Spirit (and many times spirits), and are represented in nondenominational and independent churches and ministries, and even postdenominational churches. The independents and nondenominationalists in particular fit this category because they may be influenced by classical Pentecostals or Charismatics but they do not accept the doctrine of Spirit baptism or are not members of any denomination. Theologically there is similarity with Pentecostalism, but the refusal to identify with classical Pentecostalism's distinctive doctrine and their refusal to be involved in denominationalism puts them into this separate category.

The decades of the sixties and seventies were an important time because of the increased influence of non-Pentecostal beliefs on Pentecostal thinking. Through the Charismatic movement, Pentecostals were influenced by Catholics and mainline Protestants. This resulted in changes in how Pentecostals thought about the Holy Spirit, salvation, faith, and money. During these two decades, Pentecostals were changing both how they thought and and how they lived. This was a time of great ferment. By the eighties and nineties, Pentecostalism had undergone significant changes, had become a global movement, and was predominated by churches and ministries with hybrid forms of worship and theology. I believe this is a major reason the third wave has exploded.

This approach introduces both language and categories that can assist scholars and students alike in exploring the roots and multifarious branches of Pentecostalism and the prosperity emphases. Once the movement's origins are rightly understood in the classical Pentecostal tradition, then one is able to see the movement's progression through the various strands of the Charismatic movement and lastly through the myriad of hybrid neo-Charismatic or nondenominational churches that

---

19. Anderson, *African Reformation*.

espouse varying forms of mainline, classical Pentecostal, and Word of Faith teaching. This approach also forces both proponents and critics of the movement to develop more sophisticated and nuanced mechanisms of assessing the movement's breadth and variance. Continuing to view the movement as only an American Word of Faith movement that reformulates New Thought and Mind Science is insufficient and needs correction. All Pentecostals are not the same. All brands of prosperity teaching are not the same either.

One possible way of correcting this tendency is to offer an alternative historical model that is nuanced and specific to prosperity teaching in the United States. In the following two tables, I provide a rough genealogy with three categories of prosperity teachers as a preliminary mechanism that accounts both for the historical development of the movement and theological variance. This, however, is not a model that accounts for prosperity teaching in the Two-Thirds World.

Table 2: Prosperity Teachers

Category 1: Pentecostal Pre-Word of Faith Prosperity Teachers (1930s, '50s–'60s)
Thomas Wyatt
Oral Roberts (Founder of Oral Roberts Ministries and Oral Roberts University)
Gordon Lindsay
A. A. Allen (Founder of A. A. Allen Ministries)
Ken Hagin (Founder of Kenneth Hagin Ministries and Rhema Bible Church, Tulsa)

Category 2: Word of Faith Prosperity Advocates (1970s–present)
Kenneth Copeland (Founder of Kenneth Copeland Ministries, Ft. Worth)
Creflo Dollar (Pastor and Founder of World Changers International Church, Atlanta)
Jerry Savelle (Teaching Pastor, Founder of Jerry Savelle Ministries)
Jesse Duplantis (Founder of Jesse Duplantis Ministries, Baton Rouge)
Fred Price (Pastor and Founder of Crenshaw Christian Center, Los Angeles)
I. V. Hilliard (Pastor and Founder of New Light Christian Center Church, Houston)
Michael Freeman (Pastor and Founder of Spirit of Faith Christian Center, Temple Hills, MD)
Kenneth Hagin Jr. (Pastor of Rhema Bible Church, Tulsa)
Keith Butler (Pastor of Word of Faith Christian Center, Detroit)
Leroy Thompson (Pastor of Ever Increasing Word Ministries, Darrow, LA)

Category 3: Non-Word of Faith Prosperity Advocates (1970s–present)
Morris Cerullo (Independent Evangelist, former Assemblies of God minister)
Miles Munroe (Bahamas Independent Pastor)
T. D. Jakes (Oneness, T. D. Jakes Ministries)
Eddie Long (Formerly Full Gospel Baptist)
Kirbyjon Caldwell (United Methodist)
Joel Osteen (Independent Pastor)
Jim Bakker (Independent Evangelist, former Assemblies of God Pastor)

Benny Hinn (Independent healing Evangelist)
Paul Yongi Cho (Pentecostal Korean Pastor)
John Avanzini (Independent Evangelist, former Assemblies of God Minister)

The three categories—pre-Word of Faith prosperity advocates, Word of Faith prosperity advocates, and non-Word of Faith prosperity advocates—allows the study of the prosperity movement to be divided into manageable eras, enabling one to examine the movement as it evolved from within classical Pentecostalism in the post-World War II healing revivals and the advent of the neo-Pentecostal or Charismatic renewal and independent Spirit-filled churches.

Table 3: Differing Beliefs about Prosperity among Prosperity Teachers

Oral Roberts—The goodness of God and seed faith that produces financial blessings often referred to as a harvest.

A. A. Allen—Prosperity can be experienced as a deliverance of sorts from satanic bondage. Satan wants Christians living without health and finances, not God.

Ken Hagin—It is God's will to heal and prosper and Christians can receive these blessings through one's confession in faith.

Kenneth Copeland—There are immutable laws that govern prosperity. Both healing and prosperity are covenant benefits.

Fred Price—God's original intent for creation was blessing, which meant no need. One is able to receive what God wills for all creation through active faith in the Word of Faith and promises of God.

John Avanzini—God is not poor but rich and placed enough wealth in the earth for every person's needs and wants to be met.

Creflo Dollar—Total life prosperity is the ability to control every circumstance.

Leroy Thompson—God wants Christians to have money and not to be broke. It is the love of money which is the root of evil and not money itself.

T. D. Jakes—Finance is the vessel that brings people to their destination—enabling us to go from where we are to where we are meant to be. One must position and reposition oneself in order to prosper.

Eddie Long—Christians are children of the kingdom and as such have dominion on the earth.

Joel Osteen—Prosperity is believing in yourself and that God wants you to enjoy your life.

These beliefs demonstrate the tremendous amount of variance within Pentecostalism on this subject. This table raises new questions, such as, what is it about Pentecostalism that formed the theological base upon and from which hybrid forms of prosperity teachings arose? Also, did prosperity teachers alter the trajectory of Pentecostal theology?

HISTORICAL ORIGINS OF THE PROSPERITY MOVEMENT

The prosperity movement originated out of classical Pentecostalism in the 1960s through the teachings of two popular healing evangelists: Oral Roberts and A. A. Allen.[20] Prosperity teaching actually began with them. In 1955 and 1960 Oral Roberts published the first two of a number of works that would advocate prosperity. In the first book, entitled *God's Formula for Success and Prosperity*, Roberts provided testimonials from businessmen such as Clifford Ford, Henry Krause, and Demos Shakarian, all who "prospered" applying the same teachings from the Bible used by Roberts. Ford, for example, claimed, "The Word of God gives us a formula for everything we need in this world. The three things that every child of God should have are, in the order of their importance, personal knowledge of genuine salvation, health for the body, and prosperity." And Ford concluded that "the Word of God gives us a formula for each."[21] As early as the fifties, healing evangelists like Roberts had already introduced many Pentecostals, including select businessmen, to the language of prosperity and practice of looking to Scripture for formulas that bring healing and prosperity.

Roberts also provided much of the theological rationale for prosperity. *God is a Good God* was an important work that framed prosperity as a result of a right view of God. In this work, Roberts felt compelled to deliver this simple yet very profound point. One can sense his passion from reading the subtitle *Believe It and Come Alive* and also the preface at the outset of the book.

> *God is a Good God*. This single idea, based on the revealed Word of God, is a simple yet powerful concept that changed my life and has changed the lives of millions who have accepted it. The concept is stated most clearly in the title: God is a Good God. Believe this idea, understand its all-embracing meaning and application, and your life can become a new experience in the abundance of God's gifts–materially, physically, mentally, spiritually. It is my purpose to bring this message and its vast

---

20. See Beumler, *In Pursuit of the Almighty's Dollar*, 225–26, and Bowman, *The Word-Faith Controversy*, 38–41.

21. Ford, "God's Real Estate Man," 11.

> implications to you—to seek to make it meaningful and vital to every person who reads these words. I believe—I know—it is the answer that we have from our Savior, the answer to every evil that besets our world and our lives. In my ministry in this country and in other lands, I see so much unnecessary illness, sadness, misery, so much that I know God does not want to exist in his world. I see little children with broken bodies. I see men and women tortured by doubt and guilt and fear. . . . I see poverty and hunger in the midst of surplus that is there for the asking and taking . . . I want these people to know that this does not have to be.[22]

For him, the conditions of people living in sickness, with doubts and fears, and in poverty are all related to their misunderstanding of God's will. He adamantly says, "God does not want you to be sick, or to be poor. He does not send misery and despair; he wants none of these things for you. . . . A good God could not be that kind of God."[23] He bases this claim on two beliefs. First, Roberts believes that the essential nature of God is good. God is a good God. This is a simple message but the import is significant for him. When one understands this, it can dramatically change his or her life. Secondly, he believes that prosperity is linked to the good nature of God. So, in varying ways throughout this book, he reasons that a good God only wants the best for his children. This means that anyone experiencing sickness, doubt, poverty, etc. needs to realize that this is not what God wants for them. This line of thinking will be repeated by later teachers of prosperity but it began with Roberts.

There was another important belief that began with him too. In 1970, he published *The Miracle of Seed Faith*. This book laid the groundwork for prosperity teaching. In it, Roberts combined faith, which was becoming one of most important teachings in Pentecostalism during the late fifties, sixties, and seventies, with money. What was unique about him was that he talked about money using the language of seed. Your money was a seed that could yield a harvest. From the verse in Genesis 8:22 that says, "While the earth remaineth, seedtime and harvest, cold and heat, and summer and winter, and day and night shall not cease," he deduced that seedtime and harvest were eternal principles that even Paul alluded to in Galatians 6:7. From this eternal principle, he developed the idea of the "blessing pact." The blessing pact is based on the belief

---

22. Roberts, *God Is a Good God*, 9–10.
23. Ibid., 11.

that "everything God does starts with a seed planted" and is based on three principles (1) God is your source, (2) give that it may be given to you, and (3) expect a miracle.[24] The *Miracle of Seed Faith* set the stage for other books that advocate prosperity, works like *Flood Stage: Opening the Windows of Heaven* (1981) and *Attack Your Lack* (1985). Roberts proved to be innovative in developing a beginning theology of prosperity rooted in his idea of seed faith and his belief in the goodness of God. He laid the groundwork for later forms of prosperity teaching.

A. A. Allen was also instrumental in articulating teachings about prosperity. He produced one of the first prosperity books in 1953. In *The Scriptural Secret to Financial Success*, Allen opened the book by asking his readers three questions: "Do you believe the Bible?", "Do you believe God gave every promise in the Bible?", and "Do you believe that every promise in the Bible is true?" For those who share his belief, he lists ten biblical texts, most of which come from Deuteronomy 28, that promise blessings of various kind.[25] He affirmed that anyone who believes these verses can experience these blessings. He followed that by saying, "To many people today, the heavenly windows of God's blessing are closed. Doubt, unbelief, skepticism, or perhaps lack of knowledge of God's word, have closed them."[26] He followed this book on prosperity with another one entitled *Your Christian Dollar*, written in 1958, and *Send Now Prosperity*, written in 1968.

Allen is important because later advocates of prosperity will use texts he introduced in the fifties that "promise" prosperity. For example, in the book *Send Now Prosperity*, he provided an extensive list of scriptural texts that support prosperity teaching. In fact, in chapter 1 he cites 186 texts from the Bible to support prosperity and in chapter 2 he cites 115 verses highlighting the theme of poverty and shame. Every book he wrote on prosperity quotes the Bible extensively. He provided later teachers with a plethora of verses to draw on and reinforce the belief that God promises prosperity. He is also an important figure because of his belief in the doctrine of retribution. This teaching insists that God blesses or rewards the faithful and curses the unfaithful. For Allen, this is how the world works. It is universal. Blessings come from God while poverty, sickness, and sin come from Satan and the key to receiving the blessing of prosperity is faith in God and obedience to his word. In fact his understanding of faith

24. Roberts, *Miracle of Seed Faith*, 8.
25. 3 John 2; Deut 28:2, 4–6, 8, 12; Mal 3:10–11.
26. Allen, *The Secret to Scriptural Financial Success*, 8.

is a precursor to later Word of Faith types like Kenneth Hagin, Kenneth Copeland, and Fred Price. Both Oral Roberts and A. A. Allen are major figures in the evolution of the prosperity doctrine within Pentecostalism.

While Ken Hagin Sr. is important, he followed these two influential leaders and their teachings that the nature of God is good, that giving is the key to financial prosperity, that multiple verses in the Bible promise prosperity, and that Christians live in a world where faithfulness is rewarded and unfaithfulness is not. Hagin built on the foundation laid by these two healing evangelists. In fact, Hagin was greatly influenced by Oral Roberts's teaching on healing and faith, as well as the writings of E. W. Kenyon. As such Hagin is one of the most prominent figures in the movement, providing an especially clear and pronounced theology of prosperity. Furthermore, it was Hagin who became a founding figure of a new hybrid form Pentecostalism commonly referred to as the Word of Faith movement. Hagin takes Pentecostal teachings about faith, healing, and prosperity in new directions. By publishing a myriad of books on faith, healing, prayer, the gifts of the Spirit, and prosperity, Hagin spawned a new movement that not only influenced classical Pentecostal denominations, but also a growing number of Charismatic Christians. Some of Hagin's more popular book titles include *How To Write Your Own Ticket with God* (1979), *You Can Have What You Say* (1991), *El Shaddai: The God Who Is More Than Enough* (1980), *Biblical Keys to Financial Prosperity* (1995), and *The Midas Touch: A Balanced Approach to Biblical Prosperity* (2000). As a result of his heavy influence, many in the Pentecostal and Charismatic arena left their denominations and began forming "Word" churches. These churches were considered hybrids because they retained Pentecostal worship and theology while augmenting them with the heavy emphasis on the Word of Faith teachings: faith, healing, and prosperity. Kenneth Hagin is rightly regarded as the founder of the Word of Faith movement but he should not be regarded as the founder of prosperity teaching. He adapted the teachings on blessings and finances that were taught by Oral Roberts and A. A. Allen. These ideas did not begin with him. While Hagin's heavy reliance on E. W. Kenyon has been well documented by McConnell and is not disputable, there are other influences, including his personal beliefs as a religious teacher. Also, his teachings need to be examined in light of their emergence from within Pentecostalism and not as if he developed these beliefs in a cultural vacuum.

I would argue that his beliefs about prosperity are influenced by his understanding of the nature of God. Hagin's theology about God is distilled in a small booklet written in 1980, entitled *El Shaddai: The God Who Is More Than Enough.*[27] In the introductory section, Hagin set out to define El Shaddai as one of the seven covenant names for God. El Shaddai means that God is the almighty or the self-sufficient one. God's self-sufficiency for Hagin means that God is more than enough. In the first chapter he went through the stories of God's works that demonstrate God's provision no matter the circumstance. God's provision encompasses acts of deliverance, divine protection, divine intervention, food, wine, healing, and forgiveness. According to how Hagin interprets Psalm 91, God as El Shaddai provides or wants to give. That includes deliverance, answered prayer, presence in trouble, and salvation. Interestingly, El Shaddai was not understood in terms of providing prosperity but rather a life where one's needs are met. Hagin's understanding of God can also be found in a small booklet entitled *Don't Blame God,* written in 1979. This book gives a glimpse into the personal life issues that influence his theological beliefs. Hagin admits that he was "never happy as a child ... [and] never laughed" because his father left him at the tender age of six.[28] Even worse, it seems that young Hagin was picked on a lot because he was weakened by a physical condition. Interestingly, he accepted Jesus Christ while bedridden, and his description of the kinds of questions that riddled him affected the trajectory of his theology.

> Questions arose in my mind: why was I born this way? Is God the author of the sufferings that are in this world today? I remember asking myself: who is responsible for all of this? Why me, I asked God. Why did I have to be a premature baby who weighed less two pounds? Did you cause me to be born prematurely? Why did I have to be afflicted all my life? Why couldn't I have had a normal childhood? ... Why couldn't I have known happiness? ... Such questions demand an answer.[29]

Hagin found answers in the Bible, particularly Acts 10:38, which mentions Jesus going about doing good and healing the sick. Life's perplexing questions that plagued the young and weak Hagin were answered in the final chapters of this booklet. Hagin's response is that "accidents, disease,

---

27. Hagin, *El Shaddai.*
28. Hagin, *Don't Blame God,* 4–5.
29. Ibid., 6–7.

sickness, and disasters come as a result of the fall of man. Their author is Satan."[30] He quite adamantly asserted that Jesus is the deliverer of men and women, not a destroyer. These explanations are significant to his understanding of the nature of God. Hagin does not blame God for evil in the world and uses this booklet to encourage others with questions and doubts not to blame God either. God works for human flourishing, according to Hagin.

However, two people who were particularly influenced by Hagin made prosperity a distinct focus in their ministries. Kenneth Copeland and Fred Price accepted the teachings of Hagin on faith, healing, and prosperity. As a result Kenneth Copeland and later his wife Gloria Copeland would begin teaching at "Believer's Conventions" across the nation. Both Kenneth and Gloria Copeland advocated prosperity through four key publications: *God's Will is Prosperity* (1978), *Prosperity: The Choice is Yours* (1985), *The Laws of Prosperity* (1995), and *Managing God's Mutual Funds—Yours and His: Understanding True Prosperity* (1997).

Fred Price introduced and popularized prosperity teaching in the black community. Shortly after receiving the baptism of the Spirit, Price was introduced to the teachings of Kenneth Hagin. Currently Frederick Price serves as pastor of Crenshaw Christian Center in Los Angeles, with a membership of more than 20,000. His television broadcast *Ever Increasing Faith* airs in fifteen of the twenty largest markets in America, reaching more than fifteen million households per week. Starting in 1990, Dr. Price has provided spiritual oversight to more than 300 churches through a network called the Fellowship of Inner City Word of Faith Ministries (FICWFM). Since 1976 he has written more fifty books on faith, healing, and prosperity that have sold over two million copies. Titles like *The Purpose of Prosperity* (2001), *Higher Finance: How To Live Debt Free* (1999), and *Prosperity: Good News to You* (2008) are examples of his commitment to prosperity teaching.

Copeland and Price have influenced many second-generation prosperity teachers like Jerry Savelle, Creflo Dollar, Jesse Duplantis, LeRoy Thompson, Michael Freeman, and I. V. Hilliard, who centralize prosperity teaching in their weekly broadcasts and missionary endeavors, thus spreading the influence of the movement nationally in Pentecostal, Charismatic, and nondenominational churches and globally through the

---

30. Ibid., 11.

missionary agencies and churches that have served the two-thirds world for more than half a century.

CONCLUSION

One of the things I hope to accomplish with this book is to change the way we study the movement by situating the prosperity movement within Pentecostalism. The popular belief that it is only a product of Ken Hagin—who plagiarized E. W. Kenyon, a closet disciple of New Thought metaphysics and Mind Science—is an inadequate and problematic narrative. The emergence of growth in the prosperity movement is more complex. I have tried to introduce some of this complexity by providing a careful discussion of the various strands of Pentecostalism and beliefs about prosperity among Pentecostals. I have also sought to highlight the connection between classical Pentecostalism, the emerging Word of Faith movement, and later hybrid Pentecostal and Charismatic nondenominational churches. I have done this by providing a historical narrative that began with Oral Roberts and A. A. Allen and then moved to Hagin, Copeland, Price, and others. The history of this movement begins among denominational Pentecostals but becomes prominent among nondenominational Pentecostals through the Word of Faith movement and the many pastors and ministries they influence. The emerging emphasis on prosperity in Word of Faith churches and ministries was a reformulation or an altogether new form of Pentecostalism. Word of Faith teachers like Hagin, Copeland, and Price represent a shifting narrative within Pentecostalism. Therefore, some knowledge about this shift within Pentecostalism is a significant component of this study. This is the work I will take up in the next chapter.

— CHAPTER 2 —

Changing the Narrative of American Penecostalism

A BASIC UNDERSTANDING OF the history and thought of Pentecostalism is a critical part of the emergence of the Word of Faith movement and the centrality and prominence of prosperity teaching. The prosperity movement is a product of the Pentecostal movement. As such, a discussion of Pentecostal history is important to developing an informed understanding of prosperity teaching. In particular, I would argue that the prosperity movement represents a fundamental shift in the Pentecostal movement away from the Spirit-empowered life to individual success and illustrates how a formerly persecuted movement went from obscurity to mainstream popularity. In the last two decades of the twentieth century, neo-Pentecostal Word of Faith preachers operated with a different central tenet than their classical Pentecostal forbears used in the first five decades of the twentieth century. This is the story I will tell in this chapter.

THE STORY OF AMERICAN PENTECOSTALISM

Pentecostalism, a movement that began in America in 1906, emphasizes the work of the Holy Spirit in the lives of Christians. It is named after the incidents that occurred on the day of Pentecost in Acts 2 and sees these events as paradigmatic for Christians. In the same way the Spirit moved throughout Acts, Pentecostals both expect and participate with God's

Spirit in the work of preaching the gospel of Jesus Christ with power. Historians trace the origins of Pentecostalism to events that transpired in 1901 at Bethel Bible College in Topeka, Kansas. Under the teachings of Charles Fox Parham, one student, Agnes Ozman, spoke in tongues. And they understood this experience to be a sign of receiving the baptism of the Holy Spirit. In addition to the influence of Parham and Ozman, there was the revival from 1906 to 1909 at the Azusa Street Mission, an African American church in Los Angeles. This revival had a profound impact on the origins and growth of Pentecostalism. For three years William J. Seymour held services three times a day and people from all over the world were taught about the baptism of the Holy Spirit with the evidence of speaking in tongues. One prominent Holiness preacher, Bishop C. H. Mason, the founder of the Church of God in Christ, was baptized in the Holy Ghost at this meeting.

People left the Azusa Street meeting and carried this message across the country and throughout the world. As a result, many Pentecostal churches and denominations sprang from this movement. The most prominent denominations likely stemming from this movement were the Church of God in Christ, the Assemblies of God, the Church of God (Cleveland, Tennessee), and the General Assembly of Apostolic Assemblies, which later became the Apostolic Assemblies of the World. Some of these denominations were founded before the Azusa Street Revival, but the revival gave shape to their message in such a definitive way that even they look back to Azusa Street as where it all began. Today these denominations have millions of members in them and some of the largest congregations in America have roots that go back to Bethel Bible College and Azusa Street.

WHAT PENTECOSTALS BELIEVE AND TEACH

Pentecostals have distinct beliefs. When historians and scholars discuss the core tenets of Pentecostal theology, they usually refer to Spirit baptism, speaking in tongues, healing, and eschatology.[1] This is a modified version of the older Pentecostal five-fold gospel of salvation, sanctification, Spirit baptism, and the second coming popular during the days of the Azusa Street Revival. Early Pentecostals were focused on the message

---

1. See Anderson, *Introduction to Pentecostalism*, 187–224; Dayton, *Theological Roots of Pentecostalism*, 87–172; Faupel, *The Everlasting Gospel*, 187–306; and Yong, *The Spirit Poured Out on All Flesh*, 17–30.

of salvation and subsequent spiritual experiences, like the experience of entire sanctification, that give Christians power to live a holy life and to minister to those in need. Some early Pentecostals wanted to speak in tongues so they could take the gospel to the lost, not so they could pray and worship in church. These Pentecostals believed that the gift of tongues was the gift to speak foreign languages, which would enable them to preach the gospel in all the languages of the world. They had a sense of urgency because of the belief in the imminent return of Christ. The latter days were upon the world and in the words of Joel 2, God was pouring out his Spirit. That is why pastors, ministers, evangelists, and missionaries flooded into Azusa and left to take the gospel message to the ends of the earth to prepare the world for Christ's return. Over time, these beliefs would be modified as Pentecostalism grew from being what some considered a radical sect to a mainstream popular religious tradition.

The 1940s through the 1960s was a crucial time in the history of American Pentecostalism. The evangelical church gradually became more accepting of Pentecostals. For example, in 1942, the National Association of Evangelicals invited Pentecostals to join their organization. This invitation represented progress in the movement as it became more mainstream, which would be important for key developments in the following two decades, when there was also a growing openness to Pentecostal spirituality in evangelical and mainline churches. During this time, pastors and members of mainline churches attended Pentecostal camp meetings and revival services and in turn brought a little of Pentecostalism away with them. These churches began to experiment with Pentecostal worship and practices such as speaking in tongues and healing. For example, in 1959, Dennis Bennett, an Episcopal priest, received the baptism of the Spirit and shared his experience with his church and other Episcopalians in Los Angeles. Other churches would follow suit, giving rise to the Charismatic movement or the second wave among Episcopal and Catholic churches. These events redefined Pentecostalism in a unique way, shifting its emphasis away from a consecrated or empowered way of life to receiving the Spirit and being open to all the gifts of the Spirit in the church.

As Christians experiencing the works of the Holy Spirit, Pentecostals and Charismatics share basic beliefs like Spirit baptism and tongues. They also have noticeable differences. Charismatic Christians are not likely to insist that a person has to speak in tongues, as Pentecostals in denominations would. Charismatics also draw on mainline or Catholic beliefs. This has had a significant effect on Pentecostal beliefs, some of which morphed in significant ways as aspects of Pentecostal thought were utilized in different ways than beliefs in traditional Pentecostal denominations. Charismatic Christians or neo-Pentecostals inadvertently forced Pentecostals to expand and deepen their understanding of the Spirit's work beyond the fourfold gospel framework or the doctrinal formulations of Pentecostal denominations. What it means to be Pentecostal or Spirit-filled underwent decades of change with the proliferation of nondenominationally affiliated Pentecostal churches, like Word of Faith churches in the 1970s and 1980s.

Now I want to expand on common Pentecostal beliefs in a way that illustrates how Pentecostalism influences those who experience the Spirit outside the confines of Pentecostal congregations. There are four beliefs that bind these groups together. These tenets are the active work of the Holy Spirit, a spirit-world cosmology, the primacy of experience as authenticator of truth, and Spirit-influenced interpretations of Scripture. These beliefs greatly influenced later nondenominational movements like the Word of Faith movement and other independent "Spirit-filled" churches and have given Pentecostalism both theological range and depth. Pentecostal beliefs were foundational to later teachings about salvation, faith, healing, and prosperity.

Pentecostals have a distinct understanding of the work of the Holy Spirit. They emphasize the present and active work of the Holy Spirit, particularly the gifts of the Spirit like tongues, healing, faith, and miracles (see 1 Cor 12:8–10). In contrast, the American Protestant traditions were heavily influenced by cessationism, the belief that miraculous gifts like tongues and miracles ceased at the end of the apostolic period. The Pentecostal tradition centralizes the present and active work of the Spirit in the life of the church in ways that affect how one views the world, engages it, and performs ministry. Because Pentecostalism is an anticessationist tradition, its theology reflects the strong belief in a God with no limitations. This means Christians can experience, witness, and should expect the miraculous. In Pentecostal worship and prayer services there is a heightened expectancy for divine activity and intervention. When sickness or demonic activity is suspected and when there is need, then divine intervention is sought through believing prayer, tarrying, or authoritative edicts given in the sacred name.

The cosmology of Pentecostals is also significant. Many American Pentecostals believe that the world is influenced by the cosmic power of God and to varying degrees the cosmic powers of Satan and the demonic. Pentecostals believe in the spirit world. In this sense, they adopt the cosmology of New Testament texts such as Luke 4:1–13, Ephesians 6:12, 2 Corinthians 4:3, and 1 Peter 5:8–9. In particular, the cosmos is in a state of conflict between God and Satan, the good and evil spoken of in the book of Revelation 12.[2] For example, Ed Murphy, former professor of missions and evangelism at Fuller Seminary, uses a spirit world cosmology to understand the workings of sin. The Christian life for him is what he refers to as a "multidimensional sin war" in which believers engage sin on a supernatural level through angels and demons, on a world level through the fallen structures of the world, and finally on a personal level through the flesh.[3] For Pentecostals, the spirit world influences what happens in the material world. There is no possible way to understand Word of Faith theology without the influence of a Pentecostal cosmology. Hagin, Price, and Copeland all view the world in this way.

The focus on experience informs the later theologies of Pentecostals who believe experiences with God should be sought because they are real and life-changing. Experiences such as dreams, visions, trances, and other miracles or supernatural experiences are common for Pentecostals. Experience also functions to validate or verify the legitimacy of a teaching and so has a very pragmatic and important function. The test of truth is oftentimes found in the experience one has with God. This is also why the ritual or practice of testimony is important. Testimony is not the time in worship when one gives witness to God's goodness and power. Testimony reflects a deeper concern about the importance of having an experience with God. The saints testify about their experiences of healing, deliverance, protection, blessing, and spiritual encounters and invite other worshipers to experience God in these and other ways. An experience with the Spirit for many Pentecostals is the ultimate test of truth.

Known to interpret Scripture differently than their mainline and evangelical counterparts, Pentecostals gain meaning from Scripture through the prism of their spiritual experiences. Pentecostals have a long tradition of allowing the experience of the Spirit to facilitate the hermeneutical process. In other words, the Bible is not read in a flat manner, but rather a fluid one, as the Spirit speaks and opens the mind to layers of meaning not previously available. This is a different approach than what

2. In addition to the influence of biblical texts, these beliefs are partly influenced by Dispensational thought.

3. Murphy, *Handbook of Spiritual Warfare*, 99–104.

is normative for Presbyterians, Methodists, and Baptists. Pentecostals are often criticized for misinterpreting Scripture by taking a verse out of its historical and literary context. The term proof texting is often used for Pentecostal preaching and biblical interpretation. Is this what they are doing or do they hold an undergirding belief in Scripture that informs how they interpret the text? I believe it is the latter. Pentecostals believe the Bible is not just a book but a Spirit text. God speaks in Scripture and meaning is not ascertained at the cognitive level but at the spiritual level. This means that Scripture contains layers of meaning—historical, social, personal, etc. And for some Pentecostals, it contains an inner meaning or meanings that are only revealed by God to those with ears to hear what the Spirit says or to those who are spiritually sensitive. Pentecostals like Oral Roberts, A. A. Allen, Kenneth Hagin, and Fred Price were not the only ones to believe that Scripture can be understood only through the illuminating work of the Spirit. Origen, a prominent church father, held a similar view.[4] He believed that Scripture had an inner meaning and that one cannot discern the inner meaning by simply reading words. The Spirit provides illumination into the inner meaning of the text. Pentecostals hold this same belief and often find a deeper meaning in biblical texts. Word of Faith teachers are well-known for deeper or different readings of texts.

NEW DIRECTIONS IN PENTECOSTAL BELIEFS

In the seventies and eighties, Word of Faith teachers took Pentecostal beliefs in altogether different directions. Let me give three examples. First, the focus on the experiential encounter with the Spirit shifted to a focus on the life of faith for teachers like Hagin and Price. In his book *How Faith Works*, Price refers to faith as the activator of all other aspects of the Christian's life. In fact, "everything in the kingdom is activated and accessed by faith."[5] Disciplines like love, obedience, and prayer are all rightly appropriated by faith. Price brings to the discussion a unique understanding of faith. He contends that faith and belief are different, but offers no substantive biblical or theological support for this opinion. He makes this distinction in order to substantiate a theology of faith upon which to base his views about healing and prosperity. Faith has to be

---

4. Greer, ed., *Origen, An Exhortation to Martyrdom, Prayer and Selected Works*, 187.
5. Price, *How Faith Works*, 11.

different than belief because for him, belief does not act; it only assents to the validity or truthfulness of a conviction. Belief, while good and even necessary, is not as important as faith because "it will not change your circumstances or bring results."[6] Price defines faith as "acting on what you believe."[7] In another text he defines faith as "the active dynamic power activator which releases the power of Almighty God in your life and circumstances."[8] Faith acts on what is believed instead of passively assenting to a belief. A Christian can believe God can heal, but that is mere passive assent, whereas having or exercising faith that God will heal is qualitatively different.

Second, the importance of testimony in Pentecostalism shifted to an emphasis on confession or positive confession for Word of Faith teachers. Proverbs 18:21 says that death and life are in the power of the tongue and Price and other Word of Faith teachers interpret this verse to mean that believers can speak death and life into their lives. This principle is what is called positive confession, or "name it and claim it." Victorious Christian living is connected to one's confession of faith. In Scripture, confession means to agree with or to speak the same thing, a definition that is used to support the belief that confession only agrees with what God has already said regarding the Christian life. God's understanding of the importance of positive confession rests on his interpretation of this verse in Proverbs and Mark 11:23. Price uses this text to support his belief that a Christian "can determine the will of God" for their life because belief and confession can move mountains in one's life.[9] This verse in Mark can be applied to all facets of one's life.

Price views confession as a universal law. Whatever a person says positively or negatively will manifest. He stated, "If you form the habit of saying negative things even jokingly, then where do you separate the joke from the reality? When does it get to the point where you are really saying out of your heart?"[10] As a result he warns believers not to speak anything that is negative or the devil will manifest it, an idea he deduces from Proverbs 6:2. The belief that confession is a universal law that gives believers the ability to speak anything they desire into existence is a radical concept based on two beliefs: (1) the request being in accord

6. Ibid., 18.
7. Ibid.
8. Price, *Now Faith Is Substance Evidence Hebrews 11:1*, 6.
9. Price, *Name It and Claim It*, 15.
10. Ibid., 16.

with Scripture, and (2) the ability believers have to speak things into existence. First of all, the request or what is desired must come from the Word of God. Price claims, "it is impossible for God to lie. So if God says something about me it must be true."[11] What qualifies the request is that it is in accord with Scripture, because after all, confession means to agree with God or to speak the same thing. In his text on faith Price encourages believers to "talk God talk" from his interpretation of Romans 4:17. In this text God is referred to as the one with the creative power to give life to the dead and to call (think create) the things which do not exist as if they do. Price believes that Paul is talking about faith in this text. When God told Abram that he would be the father of many nations, God was either lying or speaking prophetically and in a sense creatively about what was to come. When God made this promise to Abram, Price believes it to mean, "[the promise] is already done."[12] As long as the request is found in the Word of God the Christian can name it and claim it. For decades, Pentecostals testified in worship about God's power and blessing at work in their lives. Now there are a growing number of different kinds of Pentecostals who practice positive confession to speak blessings into existence.

A final example of this is reflected in Word of Faith teachers' understanding of healing. Healing was a major theme in early Pentecostalism and continued to be so throughout the sixties, seventies, and eighties through figures like Roberts, Allen, and Hagin. But Word of faith teachers take Pentecostal beliefs about healing in different directions. Fred Price is one example. Like Pentecostals and Charismatics, he believes that healing is a part of the salvific blessings of God. However, he goes beyond Pentecostal beliefs about healing to include the promise of walking in divine health and having the ability to be free from sickness. Pentecostals do not hold to this belief. Price holds to this belief because of his understanding of the origin of sin. The important question is the who or what behind sickness and not the sickness itself.

Two New Testament texts were instrumental in his understanding of the origin of sickness. Price alludes to Acts 10:38, which states Jesus went and healed all who were oppressed of the devil and therefore Price concludes sickness is satanic oppression. In Luke 13:11–14, sickness is again linked to demonic oppression. According to Jesus, the woman was

---

11. Ibid., 25.

12. Price, *How Faith Works*, 178.

bound by Satan for eighteen years. Therefore Price strongly believes not God, but demonic influence, is behind sickness. He sees these exceptional cases of demonic oppression in the Gospels to be the norm for all cases of sickness.

Price vehemently rejects any notion that sickness comes from God to the extent that he reinterprets the account of Job. In this narrative, God tells Satan that Job is without sin—but Price says otherwise. For him, Job suffered because he sinned by walking in fear. In addition to this, he contends that "Job's statement in 1:20 is not true. God did not take his blessings and children, Satan did. As long as Job walked in faith the hedge was up but when he started walking in unbelief and doubt the hedge was pulled down. Job did it."[13] In a similar manner, he reinterprets Paul's thorn in the flesh to support his conviction that sickness does not come from God. He corrects what Paul actually reported in 2 Corinthians 12. Price claimed that 12:7 was not true but merely "Paul's estimation of the situation."[14] He added "that Paul was a man prone to brag and boast therefore he took it upon himself to believe that the purpose was to keep him humble."[15] The grace given to Paul was not to traditionally enable Paul to endure the suffering but actually the authority to use the name of Jesus. All Paul had to do was to resist the devil and the entire situation would have been alleviated. In both texts Price goes beyond Pentecostal beliefs to support his belief that sickness can only come from the devil. He makes no allusion to the consequences of living in a fallen world or the consequences of lifestyle choices on the body. All sickness comes from the devil and can be overcome by resisting the devil in faith. So while Word of Faith teaching is connected to Pentecostal beliefs, there are significant points of divergence. These teachers are clearly taking Pentecostal beliefs in a new direction.

FROM OBSCURITY TO MAINSTREAM POPULARITY

There is another way to look at this history. The story of Pentecostalism in the twentieth century is a story of a changing narrative or a fundamental shift in its self-understanding, at least for a segment of Pentecostals, from the Spirit to prosperity. Pentecostalism has come a long way in just over

---

13. Price, *Is Healing For All?*, 10.
14. Ibid., 12.
15. Ibid.

one hundred years. It is particularly important to be cognizant of the historical roots of Pentecostalism in order to fully appreciate the advancements made by such a young movement. In the cradle, Pentecostalism was an extension of the holiness movement and higher life movements. The primary focus was on the spiritual dynamic of the Christian's life as a result of having experienced sanctification and the baptism of the Spirit. This particular emphasis in varying forms was the operative norm of Pentecostalism for the first fifty years of the movement.

However, this emphasis on the Spirit-filled life with ecstatic manifestations like speaking in tongues was not accepted by all Christians. In fact, noted Pentecostal historian Vinson Synan found that Pentecostals were maligned and persecuted for their beliefs and practices. Members of the press ridiculed Pentecostals. For example, the *Los Angeles Times* reported that a "New Sect of Fanatics [Were] Breaking Loose in the City."[16] Sometimes Pentecostals were victims of violence and imprisoned. As late as 1947, Pentecostals were targets for violent acts. In that year, a sniper attempted to kill Oral Roberts while he was preaching at a tent revival in Tulsa, Oklahoma.[17] Holiness and fundamentalist preachers and teachers were harsh critics of Pentecostalism, often referring to it as Satan or demon worship, unnatural, barbaric, and repulsive. Baptists, Methodists, Presbyterians, and Episcopalians were also suspicious and critical of Pentecostal beliefs and practices. The psychological and mental health of Pentecostals was also called into question for many years. Alexander Mackie, a Presbyterian pastor, published a study entitled *The Gift of Tongues: A Study in Pathological Aspects of Christianity*. Mackie used phrenology, which examined a person's skull to measure intelligence and character. He believed that people who spoke in tongues had some kind of disease of the mind. He went as far as to conclude that people who spoke in tongues had the same type of skulls and minds as criminals.[18] This is a very pejorative finding. As a result of such widespread persecution and skepticism, Pentecostals were usually viewed in a suspicious manner and considered outsiders to mainstream Christianity. That would soon change in the late 1950s and throughout the f1960s.

During this important time, Pentecostalism began to appeal to Christians in mainline churches. Two key events that reflect this important development were the acceptance of the movement by the National

---

16. Bartleman, *Azusa Street*, 54.
17. Roberts, *My Story*, 134.
18. Mackie, *The Gift of Tongues*, 254–66, 275.

Association of Evangelicals and the birth of the Charismatic or neo-Pentecostal movement. This newfound acceptance and appeal to the populace of America via television, tent crusades, and radio broadcasts changed the entire landscape of Pentecostalism. Now that the so-called struggle for legitimacy was somewhat over, Pentecostal and Charismatic leaders had to wrestle with their identity in new and innovative ways. Some leaders reveled in the status of persecuted religion, but there was a desire to make the movement more mainstream or acceptable. A few Pentecostal leaders would find a way to do this and forever change Pentecostalism.

The Pentecostal movement's struggle for religious legitimacy was also a struggle for social legitimacy. It was particularly important that Pentecostalism could be viewed in a different way beside "holy rolling, tongue talking, aisle running, shouting" Christians. The social pressure of being so unique and the challenge to conform to more "nonecstatic" behavior gave the movement a facelift. This facelift included less of an emphasis on glossolalia and separateness, and more of an emphasis on spiritual gifts and blessings for the victorious life here and now.

As more people began to embrace the spirituality and theologies of Pentecostals, Pentecostal beliefs took on new forms—mainly because these people were not required to subscribe to a set of Pentecostal beliefs. They were free to adapt aspects of Pentecostal thinking without joining Pentecostal denominations. This meant that Pentecostal beliefs would, by the nature of the movement, be varied and multiform as they related to beliefs about faith, healing, and money. One of the new narratives within Pentecostalism would be prosperity.

THE DAWN OF PROSPERITY TEACHING

In the decades of the seventies on through the nineties, a new movement slowly emerged from within the eclectic world of Pentecostalism. This movement altered the core tenets and identity of Pentecostalism. This new form of Pentecostalism focused people's attention on their primary truth, which no longer centered on Spirit baptism or tongues. The chief characteristic of the Spirit-filled life is now success. This will be disguised in many different ways by religious jargon. It is called walking in complete victory, the life of faith, and overcoming life's obstacles. The notion that the Spirit always helps one to succeed is at its core.

Prosperity theology generally rests on three biblical beliefs and two theological arguments that function like metaprinciples in the movement. These core beliefs resonate to varying degrees with most prosperity proponents. First of all, prosperity teachers claim that the curse on creation that resulted from Adam's disobedience as well as the curse of the law that results from human disobedience has been eradicated through the death and resurrection of Jesus Christ (Gen 3:1ff; Deut 28:1ff; Rom 5:1–11; Gal 3:10–11, 13–14). The curse has been reversed and now the children of God live under the original blessing of creation. Secondly, it is believed that the material and spiritual blessings of Abraham are now available to those who are in Christ (Gen 12:1–3; Gal 3:16, 26–29). The blessing of Abraham is holistic in that it provides the spiritual and material. Thirdly, according to Jesus the heavenly Father cares about earthly needs and desires. His children can ask God to meet their needs so long as certain criteria are met and it is reasonable to expect God to meet these needs (Matt 6:25–33; Luke 11:9–13; John 15:7–8). Thus, prosperity teachers believe God does not receive glory from the physical and material suffering or poverty of his children. If earthly fathers and mothers bless their children, why should one's heavenly Father continually allow his covenant children to suffer and lack materials things? Instead, God is understood to receive glory as a result of his children's health and prosperity.

There are two theological claims prosperity teachers make about God that guide this belief. In the book *The Laws of Prosperity*, Kenneth Copeland clarifies the dimensions of prosperity that include the spiritual, mental, and physical aspects of life. He believes God wants to prosper every part of our being. More importantly, he argues that there are universal laws in the earth and prosperity is one of them. Copeland claims, "We must understand that there are laws governing every single thing in existence. Nothing is by accident. There are laws of the world of the spirit, and there are laws of the world of the natural."[19] Thus, according to Copeland, the key to prosperity is ascertaining those immutable spiritual laws that govern prosperity and applying them to one's life by faith. And one's ability to prosper is dependent on aligning one's life with the laws and principles in the Word. The second theological argument that guides this system of teaching is connected to creation. In a chapter entitled

---

19. Copeland, *The Laws of Prosperity*, 15.

"Why God Wants us to Prosper," Price invokes the creation argument.[20] Price appeals to God's original or ultimate plan for all humans, which is that they prosper in all areas of life. Genesis 1:26–28 is used as a point of reference to reinforce his theology. From the beginning God's intent was for all creation to thrive. Word of Faith proponents draw on the creation principle to support their belief that God did not originally create a world where inequality should be the norm. Even though God's original plan was thwarted in the garden of Eden with the fall, God's plan was still evident through the lives of the patriarchs. For Price, the prosperity evident in the lives of the patriarchs proves that prosperity was God's intent, though the fall interrupted it from being fully manifested in the world. Faith teacher John Avanzini made a similar argument in his book *The Wealth of the World*.[21] Avanzini reasons if God did not want believers to be prosperous, he would not have created a world with such a wealth of natural resources, which produce billions and sometimes trillions of dollars. He listed some of the major natural resources and the wealth they will produce over the next twenty years to support his belief that God placed enough wealth in the world for every person to be rich.

- 220 billion dollars of copper;
- 50 trillion dollars of gold;
- 300 billion dollars of silver;
- 600 billion dollars of aluminum;
- 16 trillion dollars of oil;
- 1.5 trillion dollars of barley;
- 4 trillion dollars of corn;
- 19 trillion dollars of meat;
- 4 trillion dollars of rice;
- 4 trillion dollars of pork;
- 3.6 trillion dollars of wheat[22]

The problem is twofold. Christians have been kept in the dark about the wealth of the world, considering the topic taboo. Also, people do not share the wealth God placed in the earth for everyone. These biblical

---

20. Price, *The Purpose of Prosperity*, 1.
21. Avanzini, *The Wealth of the World*.
22. Ibid., 57–58.

verses and theological beliefs form a base upon which various strands of prosperity teachers build. Moreover, this new narrative for Spirit-filled Christians centered on success, well-being, and money creates fundamentally different ways of being Pentecostal and tension between the old Pentecostals and new guard Pentecostals, which introduces an additional layer to this history.

THE MONEY DEBATE IN PENTECOSTALISM

While many Pentecostals of various strands embraced this new teaching, many others did not. In fact, not all Pentecostals were happy about this shifting narrative. As a result, prosperity teaching caused a vigorous and ongoing debate over the issue of money within Pentecostalism between the traditional Pentecostals and the emergence of two groups: Charismatics and neo-Charismatics (think independent nondenominational). In *You Can Have What You Say: A Pastoral Response to the Prosperity Gospel,* James Bowers argued that prosperity teachers were using television to make significant inroads into the Pentecostal communities and that their influence has served as a replacement or rival to the educational and discipleship work of local congregations. He sought to address the pastoral challenges of this movement that was influencing Church of God congregations. This trend represented a shift in authority from congregations to television ministries. Formation and discipleship were being done by these new teachers, who were advocating different teachings. Furthermore, in his analysis of the sources and teachings of the movement, Bowers explores the pillars of Word of Faith theology while commenting on the theological differences between Word of Faith and Pentecostal theology. This yields interesting comparisons between the two belief systems.

> Values had more to do with personal success, security, and status and certainly less to do with the traditional Pentecostal themes of repentance and salvation, sanctification and holiness, Holy Spirit Baptism and tongue speaking, anointing with oil and healing, and urgent passion for the return of Christ. That is, the original "full gospel" of Pentecostal faith was increasingly displaced by a generic Pentecostal-Charismatic spirituality more acceptable to North American non-Pentecostals and Charismatic believers.[23]

23. Bowers, *You Can Have What You Say*, 7.

Bowers shows a concern that important Pentecostal distinctives are being lost with the advent of prosperity teaching, particularly tongues and a passion for the second coming. This is a significant point that most studies have overlooked.

During the early years, many though not all Pentecostals were poor and had very conservative and otherworldly beliefs, especially about the evils of money.[24] When the Pentecostal revival broke out in the first two decades of the twentieth century, Pentecostal preachers "preached to millhands in factories, to road gangs by the wayside, to workmen in railroad yards and iron works, and to farm hands in cotton fields. . . . They journeyed by wagon and horseback into remote rugged mountain regions."[25] Early Pentecostal beliefs were partly due to the fact that Pentecostal revivals broke out among poor people in places like Cleveland, Tennessee, Little Rock, and Los Angeles. There was also the heavy influence of apocalyptic beliefs: the world is evil and Jesus is coming back to judge the world. Anderson also described Pentecostal preachers as people

> who lived in extreme poverty, going out with little or no money, seldom knowing where they would spend the night, or how they would get their next meal, sleeping in barns, tents and parks, or on the wooden benches of mission halls, and sometimes in jail. Bands of workers would pool their funds, buy a tent or rent a hall, and live communally in the meeting place, subsisting at times on flour and water, or rice, or sardines and sausages.[26]

These meager beginnings persisted for many Pentecostals. For example, there were many major leaders within Pentecostalism who grew up very poor and experienced abject poverty. Oral Roberts, A. A. Allen, Ken Hagin Sr., Fred Price, Ken and Gloria Copeland, Jim Bakker, and T. D. Jakes were very poor at one point in their lives. This factor is very important.

Since large numbers of Pentecostals were poor, they had values formed by the experience of being poor in America and thought theologically about what it meant to be poor in this world but rich toward God. This kind of thinking was very much a part of the Holiness Pentecostal traditions that I grew up in. We were lower-middle-class people. It was common to hear a Pentecostal preacher decry the sinfulness of the

---

24. Anderson, *Vision of the Disinherited*, 114–36. See also Wacker, *Heaven Below*, 199–216 for a study of the good number of Pentecostals who were not poor or socially disenfranchised.

25. Anderson, *Vision of the Disinherited*, 77.

26. Ibid.

rich, sometimes to the extent of glorifying poverty as a godly virtue. We were taught that, as poor people, we were in the will of God and that the rich were in trouble. And so when Word of Faith teachers began to talk so openly about money, it created quite a stir because it was a clear deviation from the messages we had heard for years. Word of Faith teachers go to great lengths either to correct or denounce beliefs that even remotely glorify poverty. When reading Hagin, Copeland, and Price one cannot help but to detect an internal debate and belief system that they are kicking against.

Every book on prosperity written by Word of Faith teachers engages in this vigorous debate. In Hagin's *Biblical Keys to Financial Prosperity*, he gives a glimpse into the prosperity debate that was emerging in the Pentecostal arena. According to him "some folks thought it was a sin to have money."[27] Ken Copeland says, "Through our traditional ideas, we have been led to believe that prosperity is ungodly,"[28] while his wife Gloria echoes similar sentiments in her statement that "tradition teaches that poverty and Christianity are tied together with a very short rope" and "to be spiritual you should suffer want in the world."[29] Fred Price spent time refuting these beliefs in his books and explained that some "Christians are being nourished and nurtured on the idea that poverty is a badge of honor" and that "there is a disdain for (financial) prosperity."[30]

This debate between the older traditional Pentecostal disdain for wealth and an emerging appreciation of the importance of financial prosperity is important for two reasons. First, it underscores the fact that prosperity teaching originally sought to correct an imbalanced understanding of the inherently evil nature of wealth within Pentecostalism. Second, Word of Faith prosperity teachers began to develop theological language and beliefs that articulated ways that wealth could be redemptive for Christians. Hagin, Copeland, and Price, each in their different ways, argue that God originally intended for human needs to be met, that God wants to bless covenant people, that salvation has spiritual and material benefit, and finally, that wealth in itself is not evil but can actually be a tool to do much good for the gospel. In all actuality, the Word of Faith movement represents an advance of sorts about the ways Pentecostals thought about money, especially as the movement became mainstream.

27. Hagin, *Biblical Keys to Financial Prosperity*, 30.
28. Copeland, *Prosperity*, 13.
29. Copeland, *God's Will Is Prosperity*, 9.
30. Price, *Higher Finance*, v.

And there is no escaping how this movement would reorient the way people think about Pentecostals. For example, scholarly studies of the prosperity movement increasingly conflate the older Pentecostalism with prosperity-oriented Pentecostalism by referencing popular prosperity teachers who are Pentecostals, Charismatics, and/or neo-Charismatic nondenominational pastors.[31] For better or for worse, in the eyes of outsiders, Pentecostals in America are increasingly being categorized based on this very popular doctrine.

No one better illustrates the internal debate about prosperity teaching within Pentecostalism than Jim Bakker, who went from prosperity preacher to apocalyptic prophet. Bakker was a popular television evangelist in the seventies and eighties. Formerly married to Tammy Faye La Valley (Bakker), he was ordained as an Assemblies of God minister in 1964. The Bakkers got started with Pat Robertson as co-hosts of the Christian Broadcasting Network's *The 700 Club* in 1965. They were cofounders of the Trinity Broadcasting Network in 1973. The Bakkers became most popular for their talk show *Praise the Lord*. By 1974, Jim Bakker founded the PTL Club based out of Charlotte, North Carolina. This ministry was incredibly successful and by 1987, Jim and Tammy Faye had built a 172 million dollar empire. The Bakkers were religious celebrities and leading proponents of prosperity teaching.

In 1986, Jim Bakker wrote *Showers of Blessings*. In this book, he stressed the importance of giving and the blessings that result from giving. In fact, he claimed that he discovered one of God's greatest laws—the fixed law of giving. Bakker also referred to it as the law of sowing and reaping. He discussed biblical texts like Malachi 3:10–11 and Luke 6:38. Bakker believed that God wants Christians to prove him or put him to the test by giving. The Luke text assures givers that their "return in blessings will be greater than [their] giving and only limited by the amount [they] give, whether large or small."[32] Bakker believed that God wanted Christians to be happy and rich.

While Bakker's ministry was a success, his marriage was strained. Tammy Faye was abusing prescription drugs and was later admitted to a drug clinic. Jim had an affair with Jessica Hahn in 1980 and covered it up for years. Eventually this came to light in a series of surprising events. Richard Dortch, Bakker's assistant, paid hush money to Jessica Hahn to

31. Pinn, *The Black Church in the Post Civil Rights Era*, 135–39; Thomas et. al., *Black Church Studies*, 42–44.
32. Bakker, *Showers of Blessings*.

cover up Bakker's indiscretions. Some prominent pastors and televangelists became aware of this and Bakker resigned as chairman of PTL ministries on March 19, 1987. Ironically, Jerry Falwell took over the Bakker empire. After weeks and months of public wrangling between Bakker and Falwell, auditors discovered that the Bakkers' salary and bonuses from PTL in 1986–87 totaled $1.6 million. Worse yet, PTL was $70 million in debt. These events led to a full-scale investigation by the Internal Revenue Service and charges of fraud and conspiring to commit fraud for receiving $158 million from 152,903 PTL Lifetime Partners.[33] On October 24, 1989, Bakker was indicted and found guilty on twenty-four counts and sentenced to forty-five years in federal prison. While he was in prison, his wife divorced him and the Assemblies of God stripped him of his ministerial credentials. One of the wealthiest and most influential prosperity teachers of the eighties was in federal prison. These events sent shock waves through the Pentecostal and Charismatic communities and provided ample fuel to Pentecostal and Charismatic leaders who thought this movement was erroneous.

However, Bakker's story does not end with him in federal prison. While Bakker was in prison, he made significant changes in his thinking about the message he used to preach and the lifestyle he led. In fact, Bakker believed that God showed him the error of his ways, especially as it related to his understanding of the Bible. It started with an encounter with a young boy in prison who had given some money to a televangelist promising a hundredfold return. Instead of reaping a harvest, this young man's life fell apart and he ended up in prison. He asked Bakker why God did not bless him. This painful conversation, along with the cumulative effects of his own imprisonment, were revelatory experiences God used to expose these teachings and the harmful effects they had on people's lives. Bakker confessed to feeling responsible for the negative effects prosperity gospel had on this man's life.

In addition to this conversation, he had a dream and saw Jesus in it. Afterwards, he spent days and weeks reading the words of Jesus in the Gospels. What he found would have a profound impact on his thinking. Bakker found that "Jesus did not have one good thing to say about money."[34] During his days in prison, he began to see a clear disconnect between the teachings of Jesus in the Gospels and prosperity teaching. He

---

33. Bakker, *I Was Wrong*, 2.

34. Bakker, *Prosperity and the Coming Apocalypse*, 21.

came to realize that he and others were teaching another gospel based on a distorted understanding of Jesus. He said,

> By mixing the quest of money with a relationship with God, many preachers and Bible Teachers in our day have perpetuated a perversion. . . . [B]y giving the impression that God wants all of his people to be rich materially, we have diluted the true gospel and fostered upon the public a deceptively false substitute. We have been preaching another Jesus, another gospel.[35]

Jim Bakker was released from federal prison on July 1, 1994, and by 1997, when he published his next book, his message had changed. He was still Pentecostal and believed that God had given him a message to preach, but his message was no longer prosperity. In his book *Prosperity and the Coming Apocalypse*, Bakker claimed that the era of prosperity was over and that perilous times are upon us. Bakker had been given an apocalyptic message from God and wrote this book to warn the world that "catastrophic calamities are coming upon the earth," calamities such as "torrential rains, unsettling weather patterns, violent patterns, violent storms, floods, famines, droughts, earthquakes, and volcanic eruptions."[36] Interestingly, despite being a former Assemblies of God pastor with a prominent belief in the pretribulation rapture, he now rejected this tenet. Bakker said, "Jesus is not coming back before all these catastrophic calamities come upon the earth."[37] In this sense, Bakker's message was correcting two popular teachings within Pentecostalism: prosperity and the pretribulation rapture.

Because of this, Bakker referred to himself as a reluctant messenger. He knew how difficult it would be for people to receive this message from a minister who just got out of federal prison and had been a major advocate of the teaching he now rejected. He also knew that "most of the church in the United States does not want to hear an apocalyptic message" because it has become so fond of the health and wealth gospel.[38] US Christians were too attracted to this world and Bakker accepted responsibility for his contribution to this sad state of affairs. He sought to affect change.

---

35. Bakker, *Prosperity and the Coming Apocalypse*, 31–32.
36. Ibid., 6.
37. Ibid., 7.
38. Ibid., 8.

His book was actually an extension of the work he had already begun in circles within Pentecostalism that were very critical of prosperity teaching. For them, Bakker was the messenger they needed to counter the negative effects of this movement in their churches. For example, Rick Seaward invited Bakker to bring his message of judgment and critique to large crowds of Pentecostal and Charismatic Christians in Singapore, where prosperity teaching was popular. Bakker also condemned prosperity teaching in major Assemblies of God congregations like Tommy Barnett's First Assembly of God in Phoenix and Matthew Barnett's Dream Center in Los Angeles. Two points are of supreme interest. First, it is compelling that one of the major proponents of prosperity teaching in the eighties was now one of the movement's most outspoken critics. Second, Bakker abandoned the prosperity emphasis for an apocalyptic message, which was one of the central emphases of early Pentecostalism. In a sense, Bakker is coming full circle, back to a basic teaching of Pentecostalism.

CONCLUSION

Pentecostalism underwent significant changes throughout the first six decades of the twentieth century. By the seventies and on into the eighties, Pentecostalism in America went from being a persecuted movement for believing in speaking in tongues to a mainstream movement with popular evangelists on television and pastors of large congregations advocating a message of prosperity. Word of Faith teachers and the increasing proliferation of nondenominational churches and fellowships represented a changing narrative for Pentecostalism. However, not all Pentecostals were happy about the direction the prosperity emphasis was taking the movement and critiqued this message. The rise and fall of Jim Bakker and his resultant repudiation of prosperity teaching was a sign that there is more to this movement than successful television ministries and large churches. The movement lent itself to excess and extravagance. More importantly, this message raised significant theological questions about the interpretation of the Bible, what it means to be a Christian, and what it means to believe in God. Is success guaranteed for Christians if they have enough faith? Is suffering the result of a lack of faith or ignorance? And the seminal question: does God want every Christian to prosper financially? These and many other questions would be raised and interrogated by both Pentecostals and non-Pentecostal Christian scholars and ministers for the next three decades. The prosperity movement was subjected to critique and exposed for its theological deficiencies.

— CHAPTER 3 —

Is Prosperity Teaching a New Heresy?

"Prosperity Theology views the Bible through the eyes of a playboy philosopher and is self seeking and self centered to its very core."

HAROLD WILMINGTON,
"PROSPERITY THEOLOGY: A SLOT MACHINE RELIGION"[1]

"The garbage being proclaimed as the gospel by the prosperity pimps preaches capitalism as being synonymous with Christianity."

JEREMIAH WRIGHT, *BLOW THE TRUMPET IN ZION*[2]

WHILE THE PROSPERITY MOVEMENT grew in prominence, there were many who were critical of it and its radical claims. Sometimes there criticisms were extremely harsh. Beginning in the late eighties and extending into the first decade of the twenty-first century, this rapidly growing movement was increasingly subjected to judgment. One of the

1. Wilmington, "Prosperity Theology," 15.
2. Wright, in Carruthers, Haynes, and Wright, *Blow the Trumpet in Zion*, 8.

difficulties in assessing critiques of prosperity teaching lies in the fact that Pentecostal beliefs and practices have been largely misunderstood and criticized by non-Pentecostal Christians. In a similar manner to the way mainline Protestants, fundamentalists, and evangelicals responded to Pentecostalism with disdain for its beliefs in tongues and healing, non-Pentecostal Christians continue to be highly critical of Pentecostal beliefs and practices. The only difference is that the critique centers on a newer popular Pentecostal doctrine, that is, prosperity. Notwithstanding the history of intense criticism that Pentecostals have received from their Protestant neighbors, I believe the critiques they have of this movement are an important aspect of this history, so I am providing an overview of a select number of major critiques against the prosperity movement. In particular, I am going to focus on three macrocategories that I developed to assist in studying this aspect of the movement's history: (1) prosperity teaching and the Bible, (2) prosperity teaching, the influence of non-Christian beliefs, and the question of orthodoxy, and (3) prosperity teaching and the marginalized, which examines the debate of this movement in the African American community.[3]

PROSPERITY TEACHING AND THE BIBLE

In his text *The Health and Wealth Gospel*, Bruce Barron states that "bad hermeneutics represents a far greater cause for concern than any specific doctrinal deviation."[4] Most critiques of prosperity teaching often mention the problematic ways that Scripture is interpreted. In regard to the Bible's teachings on prosperity, the question is twofold: does Scripture advocate prosperity of some kind; and do prosperity teachers twist and/or distort Scripture to promote their understanding of prosperity? In this section I will investigate three critiques of prosperity hermeneutics that are specifically targeted at the flawed manner in which Scripture is interpreted.

Pentecostal New Testament scholar Gordon Fee wrote a small text based on two essays dealing with what he calls the gospel of prosperity and the gospel of perfect health. At the outset, he argues that the prosperity gospel is more a product of American society than the teachings of Scripture and believes its theology is sub-Christian.[5] More importantly,

---

3. See appendix for chart documenting theological critiques of prosperity teaching.
4. Barron, *The Health and Wealth Gospel*, 154.
5. Fee, *The Disease of the Health and Wealth Gospels*.

the fundamental problem with this teaching is the interpretation of Scripture. Fee lists four larger problems and provides critiques. The first problem is that the manner in which Scripture is read is guided by the belief that it is God's will to financially prosper all believers. In other words, this belief dictates and determines how verses are read instead of this belief being the result of reading verses on the subject. Secondly, prosperity teachers read Scripture in a purely subjective and arbitrary way. Fee does not believe that prosperity teaching is taught anywhere in the New Testament. It is based on randomly selecting texts while ignoring hundreds of texts that oppose this view. The third and fourth problems are deeper. He believes that this teaching is not biblical, and that it is instead based on a truncated view of Scripture's theology of wealth and possessions. Worse yet, it is based on hermeneutical selectivity. The critique of hermeneutical selectivity rests on two problems. First, it is based on the belief that there is a direct one-to-one correlation between good and evil. In other words, it is largely based on a strong belief in divine retribution where God immediately blesses obedience and punishes disobedience. This is very problematic. Second, it fails to account for the fact that God, to a certain extent, allows the blessings of creation to be enjoyed by the just and unjust (see Matthew 5). Prosperity teaching and its selective use of texts fails to account for the ways creation has been permeated and affected by the fall. It just ignores this point altogether.

For Fee, Scripture views "wealth and possessions as having zero value" instead of the belief that they are indicators of divine favor. He argues that in the New Testament view wealth can be dangerous, possessions are to be sold and given to the poor, life does not consist in having a surplus of possessions, and the poor should be content with food and clothing. These claims challenge the foundation of prosperity teaching and prove its system is based on the use of selective texts. These critiques are situated in a much larger problem with this movement's inability to understand the importance of suffering and weakness and its failure to address the eschatological tension latent in the writings of the New Testament.

Another early criticism of prosperity teaching's use of the Bible was given by Ken Sarles in the prominent biblical studies journal *Bibliotheca Sacra*. While Sarles takes issue with the theology of the movement on several fronts, his critiques of their hermeneutics are important. He provides three criticisms. First he criticizes these teachers' overreliance on

— Is Prosperity Teaching a New Heresy?—

inerrancy and flat literalism.[6] The fact that this belief is not challenged leads to troubling hermeneutical tendencies among Word of Faith teachers. For example, Word of Faith teachers accept every part of Scripture as equally inspired without making any distinction in regard to genre, authorial intent, and context. As a result, all texts are read and interpreted in a flat and uncritical manner. This creates a host of problems.

The second criticism or problem is the random nature that prosperity teachers use texts. Sarles describes the problem accordingly.

> Prosperity hermeneutics also leaves much to be desired. [Their] method of interpreting the biblical text is highly subjective and arbitrary. Bible verses are quoted in abundance without attention to grammatical indicators, semantic nuances, or literary and historical context. The result is a set of ideas and principles based on distortion of textual meaning.[7]

He has a deeper issue with this system of interpretation. These teachers are so arbitrary and random because of their belief in their authority as men and women of God. The almost equal authority with Scripture that prosperity teachers claim is the real problem. and leads to the practice of proof texting to support their beliefs. Prosperity teachers distort the Bible because they believe they have the authority to choose which texts reflect the message God has given them.

This leads to a third problem that actually exposes what is influencing their selection of biblical texts. This is most evident by recognizing the beginning point for prosperity teachers. It is not the text but rather their social location. Prosperity teachers, according to Sarles, begin the hermeneutical process with their American middle-class experience. That experience or ideal is equated with the divine agenda and will. Then they proceed to "baptize that experience with a handful of Bible verses that seem to substantiate what is claimed."[8] His line of reasoning leads one to believe that prosperity teaching is not rooted in the teachings of Scripture, but rather that Scripture is used to justify a lifestyle that is desired and imported on the text. Sarles is not the only religious scholar who believes that prosperity teachers use Scripture selectively to justify their beliefs.

---

6. Sarles, "A Theological Evaluation of the Prosperity Gospel."
7. Ibid., 337.
8. Ibid., 338.

In *Faith, Health, and Prosperity,* Andrew Perriman provides a balanced historical, sociological, and theological account of the Word of Faith movement. One of the chapters provides a discussion of the interpretive issues related to Word of Faith teaching, entitled "Problems of Interpretation and Theology." Perriman outlines three broad problems with the theological and interpretive approaches employed by the prosperity teachers. The persistent flaws in the movement's hermeneutic is due to the largely undeclared set of presuppositions and rules that govern interpretation, intellectual precommitments, and interpretive controls that predetermine the way Scripture is read and guarantees the interpretive outcome. Both Fee and Sarles allude to this. Perriman's most convincing indictment is that the prosperity doctrine operates as an interpretive control. Prosperity teachers rely on a small number of texts to support their teaching, the historical context is ignored, Scripture is viewed contractually, and some interpretations rely on misleading or poor translations such as the King James translation of 3 John 2.

Perriman also mentions the belief in revelation knowledge as a hermeneutical problem.[9] Prosperity teachers' penchant for resorting to the claim that their interpretations of Scripture come from direct revelation knowledge is a monumental hermeneutical problem. He notes that prosperity teachers tend to make this claim when their views conflict with traditional Christian teaching. Two even more unfortunate implications result. When prosperity teachers rely on divine revelation they view themselves and their teaching as somehow being above criticism. Beliefs and attitudes of superiority are common among preachers who do not have time to entertain the critiques of those who have not received revelatory insight. It also tends to denigrate the use of reason in the interpretive process. People are discouraged from thinking about what Scripture says about prosperity. Instead, they are encouraged to accept the revelatory teachings of the minister. He asks, "Why use or rely on human logic when God does the thinking for the believers?"[10] Perriman's insights are particularly useful because his intention is to provide concrete suggestions that will facilitate dialogue. But the problems with this system of teaching go beyond the interpretation of Scripture.

---

9. Perriman, *Faith, Health, and Prosperity,* 81.
10. Ibid.

THE QUESTION OF ORTHODOXY

One of the most consistent critiques leveled against the movement is the belief that prosperity teaching is a reformulation of New Thought metaphysics and Christian Mind Science. One recent study of the prosperity movement links it with New Thought and uses this link to argue the movement is heretical. Baptist scholars David Jones and Russell Woodbridge follow the popular origin theory of McConnell and others.

> The prosperity gospel is built upon a quasi-Christian heresy known as the New Thought movement, an ideology that gained popularity in the late nineteenth and early twentieth century. Although the New Thought movement is unknown by name to most contemporary Christians, the prosperity gospel consists largely of the ideas of the New Thought movement repackaged with new faces, new technology, new venues, and a slightly altered message.[11]

Critics of the prosperity movement attempt to establish a connection between these movements and to show the problematic nature of using New Thought to interpret verses in the Bible that talk about healing, blessings, and faith.

Their argument is similar to an article written by David T. Williams entitled "Prosperity Teaching and Positive Thinking" that was published in the *Evangelical Review of Theology*. For Williams, the fundamental tenets of prosperity theology were material prosperity, positive confession, faith, the power of agreement in faith, and health. He linked prosperity teaching to positive thinking and explored the connection with the positive thinking of Norman Vincent Peale and prosperity teachers who believed that material success is right and can be realized through a positive attitude.[12] Peale used select Scripture texts and taught people to focus on them in order to condition the mind. If the Scripture talks about healing, then a person should focus on healing and not on sickness. This act has an important function. It conditions the positive thinker to expect positive things and nurtures the desire to receive things. Once the mind has been conditioned, it then only has to tap into the power of faith that is activated by one's confession. This, for Peale, produces positive results time and time again. For him, if one's thinking is positive then it naturally progresses to the importance of positive confession so as to manifest what

---

11. Jones and Woodbridge, *Health, Wealth, and Happiness*, 27.
12. Williams, "Prosperity Teaching and Positive Thinking."

one envisions. Peale asserted, "If you expect the best you get the best and big thoughts get big results," edicts that sound very familiar to those in prosperity churches.[13] In addition, negative thoughts should be avoided. Williams believes these beliefs are very similar to core Word of Faith principles employed to expound the prosperity message, particularly the belief in the power of creative faith-filled words and the renewed mind that thinks like God. Williams calls attention to the theological implications of allowing the positive thinking of Peale to influence or determine how to interpret Scripture and how to teach people about God and the life of faith. For example, if one can think positively and confess what one wants to come to pass, that has radical implications for these teachers' understanding of God, particularly God's sovereignty.

This issue is taken up in greater detail by a prominent evangelical pastor. In the controversial book *Charismatic Chaos*, John MacArthur indicts the Word of Faith movement that he labeled Charismatic as being a false religion because it creates a god "whose function is to deliver some sort of cargo." He claims that Word of Faith theology has "turned Christianity into a system no different from the lowest human religions—a form of voodoo where God can be coerced, cajoled, manipulated, controlled, and exploited for the Christian's own ends," mentioning book titles of popular Word of Faith teachers as proof.[14] Titles like *How To Write Your Own Ticket With God, Godliness Is Profitable, and God's Formula For Success* prove their materialistic theological base.[15] He questions whether these titles reflect an appropriate way to think about the God of creation. In fact, *Charismatic Chaos* charges that this movement is borderline cultic because it shares the following cultic tendencies: distorted Christology, an exalted view of humans, theology based on human works, belief that new revelation from within the group is unlocking secrets that have been hidden, extrabiblical writings that are deemed inspired and authoritative, and the shunning of any criticism or teaching that is contrary to the movement.[16]

However, the real problem is theological. For Macarthur, prosperity teaching is founded upon a distorted and wrong view of God, Jesus Christ, and faith. For example, the teaching that God is bound by

---

13. Ibid., 201.

14. MacArthur, *Charismatic Chaos*, 323.

15. Hagin, *How To Write Your Own Ticket With God*; Hagin, *Godliness is Profitable*; and Roberts, *God's Formula for Success and Prosperity*.

16. MacArthur, *Charismatic Chaos*, 268.

spiritual laws or the teaching that God is not able to work until believers release him to do so are highly problematic and seem to indicate that God can be controlled and used by humans. He also mentions some questionable christological teachings, like the teaching that Jesus was only a divinely empowered man and the teaching that Jesus spent time in hell paying the price for our redemption to the extent that Satan dragged Jesus into hell. These Word of Faith teachers deny the divinity of Jesus Christ and exaggerate events that transpired between his death and resurrection. Faithful Christian living is also contorted by a misunderstanding of God and Jesus Christ. This is probably most evident in two teachings about faith that MacArthur argues against. The teaching that faith is an immutable law that works regardless of who uses it and the teaching of positive confession both undermine the sovereignty of God. For these reasons, MacArthur believes prosperity theology is dangerous and heretical. As a result, in the epilogue, he encourages evangelicals to confront this teaching and call Charismatics to reexamine what they believe. MacArthur's *Charismatic Chaos* and a later book written by Hank Hannegraff, entitled *Christianity in Crisis*, raised serious questions about the orthodoxy of these teachings.

During the nineties, there were an increasing number of religious scholars and pastors who were concerned with whether these teachings were orthodox. D. R. McConnell's *A Different Gospel* is one such work, in which he levied a strong critique of the Word of Faith movement.[17] In the introduction, McConnell placed the Charismatic movement at a crossroads because of its close allegiance to the Word of Faith movement. He insisted that this movement should not be viewed as an extension of Pentecostalism or the Charismatic movement. In fact, his guiding belief is that the Word of Faith movement is heretical and a serious threat to both Christian orthodoxy and the burgeoning Charismatic movement. McConnell makes his case in two steps. First, he shows that the origins of the Word of Faith movement go back to New Thought metaphysics, and second, he argues that popular themes in prosperity teaching are not biblical.

Traditionally Kenneth Hagin has been regarded as the founder of the Word of Faith movement. Prominent leaders such as Kenneth Copeland, Fred Price, Charles Capps, and Joel Osteen have all viewed Hagin to varying degrees as instrumental in the development and

---

17. McConnell, *A Different Gospel*.

growth of Word of Faith teaching. McConnell contended that E. W. Kenyon, not Ken Hagin Sr., was the founder of the Word of Faith movement. The most important aspect of this text was his documentation of the plagiarism of Kenyon by Hagin. According to McConnell, Hagin meticulously copied large portions of Kenyon's thought without giving credit to Kenyon. One example follows.

Hagin	Kenyon
The 22nd Psalm gives a graphic picture of the crucifixion of Jesus—more vivid than that of John, Matthew, or Mark who witnessed it.	The twenty-second Psalm gives us a graphic picture of the crucifixion of Jesus. It is more vivid than that of John, Matthew, or Mark who witnessed it.
He utters the strange words "But thou art holy." What does that mean? He is becoming sin . . . His parched lips cry, "I am a worm and no man." He is spiritually dead—the worm. Jesus died of a ruptured heart. When it happened, blood from all parts of His body poured through the rent into the sack which holds the heart. As the body cooled, the red corpuscles coagulated and rose to the top, the white serum settled to the bottom. When that Roman spear pierced the sack, water poured out first, then the coagulated blood oozed out, rolling down his side onto the ground. John bore witness of it. ("Christ our Substitute," The Word of Faith [March 1975], pp. 1, 4, 5, 7).	But he says the strangest words, "But thou art holy." What does that mean? He is becoming sin. Can you hear those parched lips cry, "I am a worm and no man"? He is spiritually dead. The worm. Jesus had died of a ruptured heart. When that happened, blood from all parts of the body poured in through the rent, into the sack that holds the heart. Then as the body cooled, the red corpuscles coagulated and rose to the top. The white serum settled to the bottom. When that Roman soldier's spear pierced the sack, water poured out first. Then the coagulated blood oozed out, rolled down His side onto the ground, and John bore witness of it. (*What Happened from the Cross to the Throne* [Seattle: Kenyon's Gospel Publishing Society, 1969], 44–45).

McConnell views this as not only problematic but also an indication that the origin of Word of Faith teaching is in metaphysical cultic teachings and not the revelation knowledge often claimed by Hagin. Kenyon's roots, according to McConnell, are not Pentecostalism but actually the metaphysical religious beliefs of nineteenth-century luminaries like Mary Baker Eddy and Charles Emerson. To him, this unchristian link proved the true origins as Word of Faith teaching.

McConnell also provided an insightful summary of prosperity teaching on three key points. The belief in prosperity is inconsistent with key teachings in Scripture, it completely challenges the traditional theology of the cross, and it disregards the Bible's teachings about the poor. On the first point, he began with the contention that the doctrine of prosperity has only two influences: the cultic metaphysical influence and the cultural influence which he viewed as the church's accommodation of the worldly values of America. Some of the issues he raised in this important section relate to need. He asked, "How much does one need?" because he believes Word of Faith teachers misconstrue need. Another issue raised was the prosperity of Paul. Paul appears to be a counterexample of the king's kid rule prominent in Word of Faith and prosperity circles. In the Philippian letter, Paul admitted to having experienced both abundance and lack. There was absolutely no indication from Paul that his experience of lack was somehow problematic for his faith. On the other hand, McConnell saw a parallel between the king's kid rule and the immature attitude of the Corinthians that Paul vigorously sought to correct.

The central issue for McConnell was the implications of the cross as it relates to the Word of Faith movement in general and prosperity teaching in particular. He said, "At stake is nothing less than the meaning of the central event of Christianity: the cross and resurrection of Jesus."[18] For him, prosperity teaching contradicted the meaning of the cross on multiple levels: it subverted the demand of the cross for self-denial, it reduced God to a means to an end, and it focused on the things of the world as a sign of God's approval. On a fundamental level, the claims of prosperity and perpetual health seem to contradict the central event of Jesus' suffering and death and how it gives meaning to Christian discipleship. Beyond the cross, he argued that prosperity teaching was deficient because of its understanding of the teachings of Scripture about the poor. In fact, McConnell believed prosperity teachers constructed a theology that not only rationalized the disparity between rich and poor, but also that teachers degrade and insult the poor by claiming that they dishonor God. And he charged that Scripture's warning to the rich is either ignored or greatly minimized. His analysis was leveled to prove that the movement falls outside the realm of orthodox Christian teaching.

Others would join McConnell in critiquing the implications of the prosperity gospel for Christian teaching. In *The Bankruptcy of the Prosperity Gospel: An Exercise in Biblical and Theological Ethics*, David Jones challenged the movement's teaching on the following counts: the Abrahamic covenant, the atonement, giving, and faith. Prosperity teachers have a faulty understanding of these rooted in a faulty theology and

---

18. Ibid., 178.

interpretation of Scripture.[19] Jones claimed that the prosperity teachers wrongly apply the blessings of the covenant of Abraham in material instead of spiritual terms. He believes when God promised to bless Abraham in Genesis 12, God meant spiritual blessings. Also, prosperity teachers believe that sin, sickness, poverty, and death were once and for all overcome by Jesus on the cross. That is their understanding or application of the atonement. Jones views this belief as the "second cracked pillar" of the movement. Because they misunderstood that Jesus was not rich during his earthly ministry, using 2 Corinthians 8:9, they misunderstand the meaning of the atonement. Jesus did not die to make Christians healthy and wealthy but rather to save them from sin and give them new life. Jones also mentions, "One of the most striking characteristics of the prosperity theologians is their seeming fixation with the act of giving."[20] His problem is that not only is giving overemphasized; the motivation for giving is receiving—in essence, giving to get. Jones concludes by challenging the belief in faith as a universal force by which believers attain the blessings of God. He argues that faith is "trust in the person of Jesus Christ, the truth of his teaching, and the redemptive work He accomplished on Calvary."[21]

In the concluding section of the essay, Jones analyzes the misuse of 3 John 2 in prosperity teaching. He claims, "Those who use 3 John 2 to support the prosperity gospel are committing two crucial errors, the first contextual and the second grammatical." Jones maintains it was not John's intention to articulate a doctrine of prosperity through this verse and the Greek word for prosperous is incorrectly understood to mean financial well-being when it actually implies having a good journey. As a result, both on the theological and biblical front Jones believes the prosperity movement is a thoroughly deficient system of teaching.

PROSPERITY TEACHING AND THE MARGINALIZED

There is a third major reason scholars question prosperity teaching. Many believe that prosperity teaching exploits marginalized and poor Christians. People in need are drawn to these churches as they seek to find meaning and means in the struggle against a life of poverty. But the

---

19. Jones, "The Bankruptcy of the Prosperity Gospel."
20. Ibid., 82.
21. Ibid.

problem is that people are given false promises. They are drawn to these churches because they have needs, but their needs are not always met. In one of the more negative treatments of the movement, David Williams discusses what he refers to as "the casualties of the faith message."[22] In other words, receiving prosperity by faith in God's Word or one's confession does not always work, especially for poor people. This failure occurs in two ways. Some people do not receive the money claimed by faith. Money does not always "cometh." They name it and claim it, confess it and pray for it, but it fails to materialize. Secondly, monies, which are often referred to as blessings, are not received in spite of large offerings repeatedly given to prosperity teaching churches and ministries. As a result, Williams explains, nonprosperity teaching ministries are left to pick up the pieces when the promised results fail and many lose their faith when it fails to produce. Worse yet, when this happens prosperity teachers do not provide an adequate response for these failures, often concluding that it must have been a lack of faith instead of a faulty doctrinal system.

He furthers his critique by explaining what may appear to be a problem with his reasoning. How does one explain the successes or the prosperity received by the advocates of the message? In other words, does the fact that the teaching works for some and not others discredit it as a viable theological system? He provides an engaging assessment concerning the pragmatic issue. He asserts that teachers prosper because they share in the prosperity of the organization or ministry that they oversee. For example, he argues, prosperity churches can operate a large-scale ministry because they employ the mandatory tithing principle as the key to prosperity. As a result, larger amounts of money are received and the ministry is able to grow through the generosity of the faithful. The implication is clear. Leaders in large organizations and ministries prosper through the voluntary giving of its members, while those giving do not have the same reliable base of support. If this is true, then "what works" in this system is to encourage people to support their organizational success and not necessarily that God supernaturally prospers faithful givers. Williams shows that the only ones prospering are the churches and ministries themselves.

In his concluding assessment, though Williams views prosperity teaching as heretical, he keenly alerts the church about the nature of heresy and the opportunity heresy presents the church. "The result of heresy

---

22. Williams, "The Heresy of Prosperity Teaching," 33.

is twofold. Firstly it is very naturally an overreaction to the problem, just as the pendulum will swing to the opposite extreme, but secondly the final result, although this may still be disputed, is a balance in doctrine, just as the pendulum will find its mean."[23] The pendulum effect of radical prosperity teaching may be a reaction of a position in the church in need of modification. Williams contends that there is room in the Christian tradition for a theology of material benefit. It is clear that in the absence of a viable theology of wealth, prosperity teaching flourished, leaving in its wake disappointed Christians who did not prosper. Nowhere is this more problematic than in minority communities, like the African American community, where many suffer from a lack in material needs.

In places of extreme poverty and among people who are poor and marginalized, this message grew in popularity and many found promise and hope in it. In America, blacks attend these churches in large numbers. Black religious scholars are very concerned about this movement's popularity and the large numbers of blacks who attend churches that preach this message. I too share their concern but am not alarmed because these churches are attempting to address issues scholars are behind in addressing: poverty and classism in the black community.

Poverty is one of the dominant manifestations of racism and the issue that dogs the lives of millions of black Americans. While black scholars were preoccupied with other issues and noticeably absent from black churches, they left the issue of money and classism for other black leaders to speak to, even if it meant speaking to it in ways that are problematic. I am not the least surprised by the high number of blacks in churches that talk about money, matters of economic empowerment, and both self and communal actualization. The popularity of this message among blacks was inevitable given the current economic plight of African Americans on one hand and the historic importance of the church in the black community on the other hand. The long tradition of black preachers who speak to a range of existential issues affecting blacks, vibrant spiritualities that emphasize worship, singing, prayer and faith in a powerful God who can transcend human limitations, and ministries that seek to meet real needs in the here and now has been a resource to blacks for centuries. This is nothing new. Unless the discussion about African Americans in the prosperity movement considers the larger context of economic marginalization and the continuing importance of the church, scholars will

---

23. Ibid., 37.

continue to miss a significant factor as to why many blacks are so drawn to the movement.

Many of the problems confronting the African American community are a result of the legacy of slavery and institutionalized racism that has influenced every facet of living for Africans of the diaspora from the early 1600s to the present. One of the most interesting paradoxes about the African American community is the reality that in spite of the progress made in the last forty-plus years, as a whole, the African American community continues to face inequities and injustices. At the end of the twentieth century former President Bill Clinton commissioned a study on race that would provide a broad look at both the progress made by racial ethnic people as well as a look at the challenges they continue to face. According to the Council of Economic Advisors for the President's Initiative on Race, the economic progress made by African Americans in the early part of the twentieth century has been slowed and even reversed between the mid-seventies and early nineties. The study covered population, education, labor markets, economic status, health, crime and criminal justice, and finally housing and neighborhoods. In all these areas African Americans suffer significant disadvantages and the African American community is in a serious state of decline.

1. Education:
   - Blacks continue to experience educational disadvantages. Blacks and Hispanic children are more likely than non-Hispanic white children to be poor and to have parents with lower education levels. As a result they often begin life with disadvantages related to family, financial, and educational resources.

2. Labor markets:
   - Wages of white men continue to exceed those of all other groups of workers. Studies indicate that black men's wages rose relative to White men's between the early sixties and mid-seventies but this trend reversed some times in the late seventies, and black men's pay declined for at least ten years.
   - After reaching near-parity in the mid–seventies black women's wages have fallen relative to those of white women.
   - Asian and white employees are far more likely than black, Hispanic, and American Indian employees to work in blue collar occupations. Within blue collar occupations, black, Hispanic, and American Indian employees are more likely to be found in the

lower paying, "low-skilled" occupations of operators, fabricators, and laborers rather than the higher paying precision production and craft occupations.

3. Economic Status:
   - Between the mid-seventies and early nineties, the median incomes of blacks and Hispanics were stagnant, whereas the median income of non-Hispanic whites generally increased.
   - The lack of relative progress among black families is in part due to the large rise in single-parent families among blacks.
   - Blacks, Hispanics, and American Indians have much higher rates of poverty than non-Hispanic whites and Asians.
   - Disparities in asset holding across racial and ethnic groups are large and exceed disparities in income.

4. Housing and Neighborhoods:
   - The national home ownership rate was 66 percent in 1997, but less than half of black and Hispanic householders owned their homes.
   - Non-Hispanic black households are more likely than members of other groups to live in units with moderate or serious physical problems.
   - Growing up in neighborhoods with concentrated poverty, high crime, and poor public schools is associated with poorer educational outcomes and may reduce chances of success in adulthood.
   - Whites and blacks live in more segregated neighborhoods than Asians or Hispanics.[24]

Though the areas under study range from education to housing, the root decline in the black community is economic in nature and being disadvantaged economically has implications for every facet of life: health, education, etc. This presidential study found that African Americans are losing ground and that there is cause for concern.

In light of the dire social conditions that many African Americans are facing it is no wonder that large segments find promise in black prosperity teaching churches. The opportunity to merge economics with faith is a promising combination for those who aspire to carve a brighter future for themselves and their respective families and communities. And this

---

24. Council of Economic Advisors for the President's Initiative on Race, *Changing America*, 13–22, 40–41, 60–68.

turn is rooted in a tradition of drawing on religion and faith to address inequities and injustices that goes back to the days of slavery.

Religious devotion in community has always been a powerful tool of resistance and a great resource to organize life and community. Black churches were one of the few stable and coherent institutions to emerge from slavery.[25] The church established mutual aid societies out of necessity, and these societies became the first institutions created by black people. The building of black churches was the first form of economic cooperation among black people. The church also gave birth to new institutions like schools, banks, and insurance companies. In the twentieth century, the black church gave birth to a number of black secular organizations: college fraternities and sororities in 1907, the NAACP in 1909, the National Urban League in 1911. Because of this, there is a communal tendency to turn to the church to address problems and issues that affect the community. Today very little has changed. In his study of the black church, Robert Franklin referred to the culture of black congregations as the core culture of African American community.[26] This context provides a compelling backdrop against which to view the promise and perils of a movement that vows to help people address inequities and injustices.

The church has occupied this central place because it gave disenfranchised people a sense of "somebodiness." Perhaps no one was more responsible for giving African Americans a sense of hope than the black preacher. Beginning in slave times the black preacher would affirm the value of black existence and interpret their experiences in light of the exodus event and suffering of Jesus on the cross. Black preachers giving people a sense of "somebodiness" has always been a central part of black life. Thus it is not a strange thing that black preachers interpret and exhort people on matters like politics and finances from the pulpit. Preaching on money and trusting the leadership of black preachers regarding money has always been a part of the black church context.

That tradition continues today. There are mainline churches that do not preach prosperity but proclaim what some characterize as a gospel of economic development. Churches like Allen Temple AME Church in New York, Allen Temple Baptist Church in Oakland, Canaan Christian Church in Louisville, and Friendship West Baptist Church in Dallas are examples of black churches promoting a gospel that emphasizes

---

25. Lincoln, *The Black Church in the African American Experience*, 382.
26. Franklin, *Another Day's Journey*, 30.

community development. These churches serve as the economic and developmental hubs of their respective communities. In the wake of the economic challenges in black communities, these churches provide an array of services such as senior housing, job training, and child care services. These churches located in inner city communities with large African American populations are concerned not only with saving souls but providing jobs, addressing societal ills, and creating wealth for their members.[27]

Black prosperity churches also function in these ways. I would contend that preachers like Dollar, Thompson, Long, Caldwell, and Jakes are following a long line of black preachers who seek to interpret the socioeconomic realities of black America in light of gospel. For example, Creflo Dollar responded to critiques of his teaching by referring to the needs of the people who come to his ministry.

> Most people who come to me their issue is I'm broke, I can't pay my bills. Don't tell me about a Jesus that won't help me get a better job. So by dealing with the Word showing them how to have a good attitude, how to get focused, how to operate in diligence, and how to discipline their lives, then you can change the way people think and live and have a better person at the end of the day.[28]

Dollar, one of the most prominent neo-Charismatic pastors in America, would claim that his message is so popular because it resonates with human need. He sees himself and his church responding to people who can't pay their bills. And it would seem that he is not alone. Pentecostal preachers of various kinds have been ministering among the poor and marginalized for a century. Dollar, though a different kind of Pentecostal preacher, is standing in this tradition that has a deep resonance with the poor and seeks to give meaning and hope where it is so greatly needed. However, most black scholars do not believe prosperity teachers are doing this but instead, are exploiting and hurting their congregations.

The debate in the black church regarding prosperity teaching and its effects in the African American community has been contentious. In a recent edition of the *African American Pulpit* entitled "Trends in the African American Church," Martha Simmons mentioned the growth of the prosperity movement. This trend receives a rather brief and negative

27. Ibid., 138.
28. Levs, "African American Churches Weigh Gospel Debate."

assessment. She describes the movement as focusing heavily on money and success and less on social justice and crisis issues.[29] In another popular work, *Blow the Trumpet in Zion,* Jeremiah Wright, prominent pastor emeritus of Trinity United Church of Christ, levels a disparaging charge against the movement's teachers calling them "prosperity pimps."[30] This strong charge results from the firm belief that this movement represents a betrayal of sorts of the core or organizing principles of the black religious experience. Wright levels three critiques on the movement in the black church. First, prosperity teaching operates as if it lives in a cultural vacuum. Second, it preaches capitalism as being synonymous with Christianity. These two critiques lead to the final criticism. Because prosperity advocates ignore its connection to a capitalistic society, they neglect how capitalism in America was built by slave labor and continues to thrive by oppressing the two-thirds world. For Wright, black prosperity preachers' failure to unpack the significance of slavery is deplorable. How can black preachers forget how their ancestors were enslaved to build an unjust economic system? How can they be content to "prosper" themselves in a system designed to exploit the weak, many of whom are their sisters and brothers? Faithful preaching cannot be "cut off from the culture that produced it and the culture that produced us." As a result, instead of following the prosperity teachers accommodationist tendencies, those who really want to honor their heritage must make the critical distinction between philosophies and practices in culture that needs correction (capitalism) from those that are worthy of acceptance (African culture).

Renowned Stanford University ethicist Robert Franklin made an alarming charge against this movement when he wrote that the prosperity movement is "the single greatest threat to the historical legacy and core values of the contemporary Black church tradition."[31] This alarming statement rests on his belief that this movement poses significant dangers for the future of the black church. Franklin argues that the prosperity emphasis represents a shift of commitments away from love, service, and justice and consequently poses not only a new threat for black clergy but a broader crisis of mission in the black church. It is in the context of this crisis of mission that Franklin offers such a strong rejection of black prosperity churches.

---

29. Simmons, "Trends in the African American Church."
30. Wright in Carruthers, Haynes, and Wright, *Blow the Trumpet in Zion,* 8.
31. Franklin, *Crisis in the Village,* 112.

First, the movement's teachers tend to focus on institutional well-being at the expense of serving the vulnerable. Second, prosperity teachers deliberately suppress, ignore, and/or delete language about radical sacrifice for the sake of the kingdom. Third, the bishops and pastors of prosperity operate as spiritual entrepreneurs who know how to produce, package, market, and distribute user-friendly spirituality for the masses. Finally and also somewhat connected to the aforementioned critique, the teachers rarely make stringent ethical demands because their primary concern is to market and distribute products.

The prosperity movement is a betrayal of the core principles of the black religious experience on several fronts. It subverts the principle of liberation and justice by its failure to address systemic and structural inequality. It prioritizes individual attainment over communal and social responsibility. Ironically this movement can only thrive in the presence of social amnesia. For example, some black prosperity preachers believe that blacks are somehow already in the promised land, which does not resonate with the social realities of most black Americans. On a more fundamental level the movement fails to deal with structural inequalities and social issues. It also fails to connect prosperity with pressing social concerns in the black community and is rarely understood in terms of providing an agenda for social change or advancement, but rather serves as a tool for individual betterment.

THE MAIN PROBLEMS WITH PROSPERITY TEACHING

Scholars and leaders from various Christian traditions have offered critiques against the prosperity movement because of theological inconsistencies and errors. I have attempted to categorize and summarize some of the major issues consistently alluded to by these leading Christian thinkers: problematic ways prosperity teachers interpret the Bible, problematic connection to non-Christian beliefs, doctrines that are believed to be heretical, and the belief that prosperity teachers do not address the issues that really cause suffering among minority communities. As a result, religious scholars draw a range of different conclusions about prosperity teaching and why so many people are drawn to it. They believe prosperity teaching represents an accommodation to a capitalistic and consumer culture. Therefore, people are drawn to it because they are uncritical of these destructive forces. They also believe the movement is popular because people are ignorant of what the Bible really teaches about God, blessings, and finances and are ignorant of the real roots of the movement in New Thought and Mind Science. So they write to educate and expose these teachings in hopes of opening people's eyes to what this movement really is, which is a popular heresy.

On a deeper level, there are four major problems with prosperity teaching. First, the movement rests on a problematic understanding of God and erroneous views about the Christian life. In prosperity theology God can be bound by spiritual laws and commanded to bless "faith-filled" believers. Theologians are particularly troubled by the absence of the sovereignty of God in prosperity theology. In addition, God in prosperity theology is almost always only benevolent and no longer uses suffering or sickness for pedagogical purposes. God's plan in creation through his covenant, the giving of the law, and the advent of Jesus Christ in prosperity theology all served to give "believers" access to the wealth of this world spiritually and materially. What is noticeably absent is a theology of glory. In traditional Christian theology, the chief end of humanity is to glorify God regardless of one's spiritual or material condition. But in prosperity theology God is the means to an end, which is to be prosperous. On some level this system seems to be wrongheaded in its understanding of God. On an equally troubling level, the Christian life in prosperity theology has undergone significant and unfortunate changes. The Christian life is measured by blessings or prosperity. In the absence of prosperity Christians are left with a deficient faith seeking explanations why God has not come through for them. There has been a great deal of concern voiced over this issue. When the movement centralizes success as a sign of divine favor those left on the outside often lose their faith altogether. The traditional Christian belief that emphasized giving to others has turned in this system to receiving. But prosperity advocates rarely offer sophisticated theological, economic, and social explanations for why the message may not work for them. As a result "believers" keep waiting for a breakthrough or again lose their faith.

Second, prosperity teaching is charged with being flawed because it misinterprets many biblical texts and randomly chooses texts to supports it beliefs, i.e., it proof texts. Teachers in this movement have demonstrated the profound need to employ more sound hermeneutical methods. Too often the Bible is not interpreted in a consistent manner but rather individual texts are used to justify beliefs that are largely inconsistent with the story of God's love and redemption in Scripture. Biblical scholars often mention two problems: the tendency to proof text and the failure to recognize genre and/or context in the various passages marshaled to justify prosperity theology. What Scripture meant in antiquity and how these texts were understood in Christian history have absolutely no bearing on the interpretive efforts of prominent prosperity advocates. Because many of these teachers receive truth through special revelation, they do not see the need or importance of interpreting Scripture in this manner.

Fee, Sarles, and Perriman all took issue over how texts were being misconstrued, particularly that the contextual concerns seemed to predetermine how Scripture is read and interpreted. As a result they found that the Word of Faith prosperity doctrine functioned as a hermeneutical control that guarantees the interpretive outcome. But I am not sure if this critique is fair. What I have found is that in all traditions, some guiding or controlling hermeneutic determines how texts are read and interpreted. In the case of Word of Faith teaching, the three pillars of faith, healing, and prosperity serve as interpretive parameters and guides for these teachers. Their guiding belief that God desires to heal and prosper those who believe and receive this by faith determines how they read Scripture. That is not a significant difference from how progressives use the belief in justice to determine how they read individual verses in Scripture or how Holiness Pentecostals use the belief in God's holiness to determine how they read texts. Critics of the prosperity system of hermeneutics need to be more forthright about the ways all traditions read and interpret texts. To a certain extent, what prosperity teachers are doing is not new or problematic. What is problematic are the interpretive ends, not the means of interpretation.

These scholars also offer appropriate challenges to a practice that is widespread within global Pentecostalism. The belief in divine revelation complicates biblical interpretation. While there is a long tradition of receiving some guidance by the Holy Spirit, prosperity teachers insist that their interpretations are the product of divine revelation. Sarles and Perriman pointed out this problem, as we saw in the preceding section. There are at least four problems with this practice: (1) it is radically individualized, (2) teachings received by divine revelation have been proven wrong in the past among these teachers, (3) it undermines the importance of using reason in the interpretation of Scripture, and (4) teachers who receive these revelations consider themselves to be beyond criticism. In addition, how does one engage in a critical conversation over how a passage or verse of Scripture has been interpreted when the person supposedly received the interpretation directly from God?

It is a common practice among Pentecostals and Charismatics to receive illuminating and revelatory insight into Scripture. It is also commonplace to receive inspired authoritative messages from people operating in the prophetic Spirit. The only possible safeguard to this practice is to deconstruct the radical individualization of the process. In other words, if interpretation and the reception of divine revelation becomes a communal process, then there can be some accountability. After all, local Christian communities give these "revelations" authenticity and authority, and so it is fitting that accountability is shared.

There are, however, some real problems with prosperity teaching, particularly in relation to its use of Scripture. For example, Bruce Barron's introductory statement that hermeneutics may be the substantial problem is an accurate assessment. There are three practices that impose serious problems. Prosperity teachers completely ignore the historical context, the teachings do not rely on a broader biblical base, and Scripture does not measure and correct its teachings. Instead Scripture is used to propagate and defend the system. While many in contemporary scholarship discredit the search for authorial intent and history controlling interpretive meaning, few completely ignore the historical context of the biblical writings like prosperity teachers. Historical context is important because it confines the range of possible meanings in a helpful way. Because prosperity teachers ignore the original context they are free to launch into interpretations that have little to nothing to do with the historical occasion. In this sense they can make the text mean whatever they want it to. Unfortunately that is why Mark 11:22 and 3 John 2 become universal principles upon which positive confession and prosperity are based. Another related problem to this practice is the failure of these teachers to base their system upon a broader representation of the biblical witness. Instead of selecting texts randomly why not base prosperity teaching upon larger chunks of passages in every book of the Bible? Such a measure can prove the veracity of the system or expose its blind spots and errors. Finally, though Scripture is quoted in abundance it is not given opportunity to correct errors in prosperity thought because it lacks authority. Scripture is a tool used to support prosperity belief but it is not allowed to function as canon, as the rule of faith. In other words, Scripture is not a tool used by the Spirit to correct. It is here where the break with traditional Christianity is most profound. Biblical texts like

Deuteronomy 28:1, Joshua 1:8, Psalm 1:1–3 and 119:11, Matthew 4:4, and 2 Timothy 3:16–17 seem to suggest that God gives Scripture and uses it to shape, correct, and perfect Christian spiritually. This function appears to be missing.

In many of the foregoing critiques of the movement's use of Scripture, the overriding assumption is that prosperity teachers distort, twist, or completely misunderstand what Scripture teaches about prosperity. It is almost as if historians and theologians have failed to recognize the abundant references in Scripture to various aspects of prosperity. Instead of the issue being that the movement's advocates completely distort Scripture, it would be helpful to focus on how Scripture functions. One who is historically informed and theologically trained knows that the Bible can give mixed signals on issues. Scripture can affirm and deny many teachings and beliefs like those related to war, slavery, women in ministry, etc. Many times the core issue is not whether Scripture teaches something because Scripture can be used to justify any belief system, but rather how Scripture is used in a particular tradition or movement. Hopefully this project will introduce that category into the conversation. The problem is not that the prosperity system is "nonbiblical" or "unscriptural," as conservative fundamentalists and evangelicals have noted, as much as it is an absence of a deliberate and legitimate hermeneutical system or the presence of a faulty hermeneutical system. Hermeneutical principles are needed that help advocates and enemies of the teaching to adjudicate the legitimacy of the system's use of Scripture.

Third, the prosperity movement's theology of giving is problematic and distorted on many levels. Some prosperity preachers and teachers encourage people to give to God and the church for the sole purpose of getting blessings. Preachers attempt to stir up the faith of the people so they will give. They tell their congregations that if you give to God you will get more back than you gave in the first place, often using Luke 6:38. Now many times they do this because people will spend money on everything except the work of ministry in the community. They will spend seventy dollars on clothes to wear to church and then put two dollars in the offering plate while complaining that all the church wants is your money. I sympathize with pastors who struggle to keep people plugged into ministry and willing to commit finances to this work. But using texts, in particular texts that make a promise of blessings to those who give in an imbalanced way, is wrong and has created a culture in churches where people give for the wrong reasons. Preachers should steward the worship of God in giving in a more responsible manner than they have in the past two or three decades. There has been little care given to what motivates giving and more of a concern with getting an offering by any means necessary, even if it means playing to human self-interest and greed.

In prosperity churches, giving is the key to prosperity and being blessed. In fact, one cannot prosper without giving money. Yet for too many, the motive for giving is not a gracious response to God but rather giving in order to receive. Some prosperity preachers cheapen the sacred nature of giving with heavy-handed fund-raising tactics and deceitful uses of biblical texts to justify raising large sums of money for ministry efforts. As a result, these prosperity preaching churches have turned the sacredness of giving to God into a cheap transaction—or worse yet, a way to manipulate God to get even more money. In the end, generosity is not a form of worship to God who owns everything, but rather an opportunity for people to get more "stuff."

Fourth, minority scholars are so critical of this movement because of its refusal to do systemic analysis when talking about poverty and other forms of suffering. This is clearly a major problem with this brand of teaching. Prosperity teaching ignores the legacy of slavery and racism and the multifarious ways it continues to impact people's lives, which is a major oversight and a serious detriment to helping people understand why there is poverty in this country and why people of color struggle with poverty and unemployment. The language of obstacles of faith, trials and tribulations, and satanic and demonic attacks, while well intended and applicable in some sense, is very limiting and oftentimes distracting because it keeps people in ignorance about the machinations and systems of the world. The language of faith in the Bible should be a guide and tool for people to understand their world, not to escape it or live in ignorance of how it works. Slavery and racism have everything to do with the current plight of the African American community and teachers need to help their congregations understand the impact of slavery and racism instead of talking about demons binding their blessings and closing doors. Churches need to know how many generations of white and black Americans benefitted from and lived under the system of slavery. Then they need to compare them with the generations of whites and blacks who have lived in the postslavery era. They need to assess, in some way, both the economic benefit and impact of slavery on white and black Americans. Churches also need to be informed about every wealthy institution, such as banks, universities, and denominations that benefitted from centuries of slavery. This is the only way to really understand wealth in America.

Prosperity teachers give an insufficient amount of time talking with their congregations about economic, political, educational, criminal justice, and religious systems and how they affect the lives of blacks. They fail to have nuanced discussions about how systems socialize African Americans into lifestyles of poverty, exploitation, and disenfranchisement. Decisions made in Washington, DC and boardrooms across the country have a major impact on the quality of life of people of color and too few teachers of prosperity educate their congregations about such matters. Instead the focus is on God doing everything for them in response to their prayers, confessions of faith, fervent worship, and financial gifts made to the church. God is supposed to shower the faithful with blessings. While well intended, messages like this will not lead to lasting change because, without systemic analysis, it only applies a Band-Aid to deep social wounds inflicted upon people for generations, which is why this movement has not resulted in a revitalization of poor inner-city and rural communities.

CONCLUSION

In an essay mentioned earlier, David Williams discussed how even heresy compels the church to clarify and articulate a more orthodox position on a theological issue. He viewed the prosperity movement as another heretical one that compels the church to develop, clarify, and articulate a theology of prosperity for the church. Maybe this is what is needed in the next few years, a theology of prosperity. If this is the case, this work is one important step toward developing such a theology. I have provided a template that delineates the issues at stake, highlights the theological fault lines in the popular movement's theology, and briefly suggested areas where there is promise or benefit. An attempt to construct a theology of prosperity or an attempt to find more positive aspects in the movement's theology must, at some point, engage some of the issues introduced here. In the end, if religious scholars and particularly its theologians develop a more balanced theology of prosperity that interprets Scripture in a more responsible manner, then they will partly owe such a theology to the very teachers and teachings they believe were problematic and heretical.

— CHAPTER 4 —

Is Prosperity Teaching Good News to the Poor?

THERE IS MORE TO the study of a movement than what's wrong with its teachings, but sadly too many studies stop there. They erroneously conclude that once people see the movement as they portray it, they will denounce their allegiance and join the right church or accept the right approach to interpreting the Bible's passages on money, giving, and blessings. The truth is, people have not stopped attending prosperity churches, even after the economic collapse of 2008, which some scholars thought would be the death knell of this movement. After two-plus decades of religious scholars and prominent leaders critiquing this movement, millions of people around the world still attend these churches and sometimes are willing to stand in line for hours to get a seat. The question is, why? Religious movements and their attendant traditions appeal to people because, among other things, they give them meaning and hope. The prosperity movement does this for a variety of people, particularly those who struggle to make ends meet in this country and countries around the world. What these teachers promise and the God they claim to represent seems to resonate with a deep need in millions of people who attend these churches and worship this God with all they have. How this movement touches the poor and is a product of the poor, even wealthy and popular teachers like Roberts, Hagin, and Jakes, who were very poor at points in their lives, should direct the study of this movement. This is a driving question in my study of the movement and others have also examined this movement's appeal among the poor.

Scholars are concerned about the poor and marginalized and see the movement as hostile to them. But their critiques, while important for a variety of reasons, have a methodological flaw that prevents them from giving this movement the careful attention it needs as it relates to the poor. It is best to see the flaw by describing the errors that pervade the study of the movement. Studies make two errors that are far too common for any movement or teaching related to Pentecostalism. First, because they tend to view prosperity as a monolithic, popular, and secular movement, they completely miss the variance among Pentecostals as it relates to beliefs about divine blessings. Pentecostals, Charismatics, and the millions of neo-Charismatic Christians all over the world have a wide range of beliefs about prosperity. Most studies focus entirely too much on well-known preachers like Creflo Dollar, Fred Price, and T. D. Jakes, while giving no attention to the contours of local and indigenous teachers who teach variant forms of prosperity. Second, studies portray people who attend these churches and subscribe to this form of teaching as mostly victims of opportunistic, predatory, and exploitative preachers and teachers, or as victims of unjust and inequitable economic system. Scholars portray people in these churches as victims and not moral agents.

These errors affect the way this movement is studied and results in a one-sided view. There is so much more to this movement. Scholars and popular pastors almost lead people to feel sorry for those dumb Pentecostals who don't know how to interpret the Bible and are so disenfranchised by the system that they turn to opportunistic and greedy preachers like Fred Price, Creflo Dollar, and T. D. Jakes, who feed on their ignorance and exploit them. This narrative of victimization and the preoccupation with popular prosperity teachers and forms of the teaching causes us to miss the strands of prosperity teaching in poor and marginalized communities. There is a broad and deep resonance of this message among the poor as well as in the larger history of Pentecostals among the poorest of the poor, which is a critical part of the history of the prosperity movement. And on a deeper level this movement touches on the issue of human need and suffering among those who have not experienced the so-called "American Dream" but instead languish in poverty and struggle to make ends meet. These people want better lives and draw on the resources of religion for meaning and answers.

I believe religious scholars and leaders need to respect the agency of Pentecostals, many of whom are poor and/or working-poor Americans, rather than root the historical narrative in a methodology that caricatures and victimizes Pentecostals who attend these churches and subscribe to this form of teaching. Scholars need to probe the reasons this religious movement speaks to the poor's existential, social, and spiritual needs. They need to study the systems of belief, congregations, and ministries that these Pentecostals construct to support their communities and they need to do it in more contexts than just large megachurches in places like Atlanta, Dallas, and Los Angeles. Such an approach is largely missing in most studies of this movement.

The prosperity movement is not just about large churches in Atlanta and Dallas. It is about poor people in rural communities who believe in God, want a better life, and are a part of the changes going on in the larger Pentecostal world. It is about the poor black preachers who preach forms of this message to others in similar situations. The movement is about the poor preaching to the poor about a better life. It is also about middle- class blacks who have it better than the poor, but are still a few paychecks away from poverty themselves. They want a better life too, and they want preachers who resonate with their experience and desires. These mid- and lower-profile pastors preach prosperity as a way to model excellence and advancement. They may be poor, but they don't have to live as and have the mentality of the poor. They reject mediocrity and victimization. The movement represents a better life. The resonance of this movement lies in the fact that even high-profile leaders like Jakes and Dollar intimately know the experience of poverty. Since God does not show favoritism they expect God to bless them too. I turn now to this context because it is where I came from. Before I ever became a religious scholar, I attended a nondenominational church that was at the center of these changes brought on by the prosperity movement. And this church had a positive impact on my life. I am not rich, but my life and the lives of others have been enriched by some of the lessons I learned in this church.

PROSPERITY

Preaching in a Rural Context

From 1997 to 1999, I was a member of an African American nondenominational church in West Virginia, one of the five poorest states in the country, with African Americans constituting only 3.6 percent of the population.[1] Poverty is a major problem in the state, especially for black Americans, and its effects are widespread and varied. Some 17.6 percent of people in the state live below the poverty line.[2] In addition, this state ranks third highest among states in fair to poor health status, fifteenth highest in having citizens with no health care access, and seventh highest among states with people who cannot afford medical coverage. Poverty touches almost every part of these people's life. It is extremely difficult to make a good living in small towns like Bluefield, Welch, Princeton, Beckley, and larger cities like Charleston and Huntington, all of which have higher concentrations of blacks than other parts of the state.

I lived in Bluefield while attending Redeeming Life Christian Center (now Faith Center Church). The African American population is concentrated in the poorer parts of Bluefield and Princeton. They work low-wage jobs with the exception of few professional blacks who teach; they work at banks, run grocery stores, and work in other professional fields. The railroad and coal mines were good jobs for men in the seventies, but by the late eighties and nineties those jobs were scarce. Unemployment is rampant. I saw more black males whose job was selling drugs or hustling to make $10 or $20 than I saw work a steady job. Hustling is a colloquial expression used in project housing complexes in our region. It stands for folks who took on any job to make a few dollars, from driving someone to the store to washing or fixing broken-down cars. There are two project housing complexes in the area. Most residents receive government aid like food stamps, and crime is a real problem. Residents not living in the projects live in neighborhoods with some nice homes as well as homes that are not as nice. In fact, some of the neighborhoods are filled with dilapidated and condemned houses. In some parts of West Virginia, people live in neighborhoods we call "hollows," though it's often pronounced "hollars." Hollows consist of two rows of houses on a dead-end street that runs back into the crooks and bends of the forest. Some very impoverished people live in these hollows. I spent the first seven years of my life in one.

Hopelessness is real in this region because people feel they have few options for success. It can be depressing just driving around town seeing all the businesses that are closed and houses that are empty. It can be

---

1. "State and County Quickfacts."
2. "West Virginia Vital Statistics Summary."

discouraging trying to find work so you can take care of your family. According to one study, West Virginia has the tenth highest rates of depression in the country, with 1 in 3 residents in rural areas experiencing a high level of depression symptoms.[3]

There were a plethora of ways blacks sought to respond to such dire conditions. Family bonds are one of the resources drawn on to combat marginalization. I have a big family. I grew up in a household of nine: father, mother, six sisters, and myself. And there were quite a few black families with three, four, or five or more kids. The region is connected by large extended-family networks. Many people feel connected to one another and the region because familial bonds run so deep. Such networks offer support like assistance finding jobs, short-term loans, help when a car breaks down, a babysitter for your kids, other kids to talk to and play with, and protection from dysfunctional factions of people in parts of the community. For example, some parents realized that the region offered no opportunity for their children to thrive, so they sacrificed and invested heavily in their children's futures in order that they could leave the region. These parents encouraged and sometimes pushed their children to excel in academics or sports as a way out. One could say they lived for their kids to succeed.

Participating in various forms of leisure is an important coping mechanism. Food takes a central role in leisure. There are cookouts at city parks and in backyards, and restaurants thrive in the region because people love good food and fellowship. This is also one reason rates of obesity are so high in the state. People fish and hunt to relax. They also love sporting events, particularly high school football. These games are well attended and loyalties run deep. There are, however, other forms of leisure in the community. The weekends in the projects are festive and the air echoes with loud music, laughs, and cursing as blacks seek a release from the pressures of the week. There is always a party somewhere. These weekend celebrations are almost ritualistic for these nonreligious blacks. Some groups of blacks turn to alcohol abuse, recreational drugs, illicit sex, and violence. The darker side to community life is a constant. Reckless sexual activity and fighting that sometimes leads to arrests or hospitalizations are almost always connected to alcohol abuse and drug use. Members of the community try to fight this evil to no avail.

---

3. "Ten Most Depressing States in the U.S."

Another response is the turn to religion and God. Blacks in this region are very religious and devout in their beliefs. They worship at church weekly and many times attend church up to three times per week. The churches vary in style, from traditional and conservative Baptist churches with hymns and prayers to nontraditional and conservative Pentecostal churches with shouting and running. The Pentecostal churches are mostly denominational of some kind, such as the United Holy Church or Church of God Holiness, Incorporated. Baptist and Pentecostal roots of various kinds run deep. Relationships between churches are generally respectful but at times antagonistic. Doctrinal differences over baptism, spiritual gifts, and women in ministry divide people in these churches, but what seems to bind them together is a love of good music. In fact, music is about the only thing that ca bring disparate groups of Christians under the same roof. There is no shortage of gifted singers and musicians in these churches. I grew up in a church with a plethora of musicians: guitarists, drummers, saxophonists, and organists who could play any gospel song by ear. Despite different styles they all basically hold to a belief that faith in God is important and that Christians are supposed to be faithful to God. They expect faith and faithfulness regardless of one's condition. I would describe these churches as very traditional. One of the popular songs in churches during this time would confess, "I'm coming up the rough side of the mountain and I'm doing my best to make it in." This song and the people who sang it in church reflected the mentality of many in denominational churches who viewed life as a struggle, and the goal was to make it to heaven. But by the late nineties these denominational churches were largely unable to speak to a growing number of blacks influenced by middle-class aspirations and televangelism. The world around them was changing and they wanted to keep up. They also wanted a piece of the good life they saw on television. They rejected as irrelevant the brand of Christianity that forced them to accept a life of suffering and poverty.

THE MINISTRY AND MESSAGE OF PASTOR FRED BROWN

The pastor of Redeeming Life Christian Center preached prosperity to the middle-class and poor blacks like myself. While I did not agree with all aspects of the message, it was empowering to hear it. It was good news in a very depressing region in the country. We were not just told that God wants us to be rich or that money would drop out of heaven to us. We were taught that we are God's children, that it was not God's will for us to languish in poverty, and that we could have a better life. We didn't have to accept a miserable life but could have good things in this world. Our pastor modeled this lifestyle by living in a nice home and driving nice cars and taking care of his credit.[4] More importantly, he used his blessings to help others. He would bless people with money, take people out for a dinner they couldn't afford, and lay before people like me an honest path out of poverty. We used the language of blessings and prosperity and our understanding of them encompassed the spiritual and material aspects of life. This was a very radical message in this region because quite a few black churches taught that we shouldn't expect better in this life and that God wasn't concerned with such matters. They taught that worldly things pass away and Christians should focus on spiritual blessings like salvation, a close walk with God, prayer, and a moral life. The pastors of these churches were very critical of what they perceived as a liberal and heretical church, often referred to as a cult by local Baptist and Pentecostal ministers. I was living in government housing, on food stamps, and struggling to find a job because employment was so scarce. I found hope at Redeeming Life Christian Center. Hundreds of other people did as well.

This church grew rapidly and became one of the largest and most influential churches in the region. Redeeming Life Christian Center is one of those hybrid neo-Charismatic churches that were becoming increasingly popular in urban centers and rural communities nationwide. It is a part of the Pentecostal tradition but is not connected to a Pentecostal denomination. The pastor grew up in a United Holy Church in Anawalt, West Virginia but attended Rhema Bible Training Center. So his church is a unique blend of two traditions within the larger Pentecostal movement. This church is very dynamic and unique. A key part of the history of this movement is that increasing numbers of poor and marginalized blacks chose these churches, with their Pentecostal spirituality, to speak to their existential plight as well as provide meaning and hope to their lives and communities. And this choice in some way was a rejection of traditional

---

4. There is a tradition in the black community of clergy driving nice cars. Prosperity preachers are not the first to drive nice cars. In the Pentecostal Holiness churches I attended in Virginia and West Virginia it was common for pastors to drive Lincolns or Cadillacs or really nice Fords. What distinguished prosperity preachers from these more traditional pastors was their choice of cars. They chose Mercedes and BMWs instead of Lincolns and Cadillacs.

teachings in Baptist and Pentecostal denominational churches, which seemed resigned to telling blacks to accept their place in society and be faithful to God, who will bless them spiritually or eternally.

In the face of dire social conditions, many African Americans in this region found promise in this black church that espoused the prosperity doctrine. Prosperity teaching churches offer five things that seem to connect with African Americans in a deep way. The first is a God who cares about spiritual and material well-being. The second is a spirituality that emphasizes personal piety and social progress. Third is a faith that centralizes personal agency (autonomy). Fourth is a belief in change and advancement in life as a result of faith in God and works in the world. Fifth is a holistic vision of salvation that encompasses forgiveness of sin and restoration to new life in this life and the next. These beliefs resonate with middle-class and poor blacks and draw them to prosperity churches with their rich Pentecostal spirituality.

What does this theology look like and how is it different from more traditional black churches? Black prosperity churches like Redeeming Life Christian Center lay out a distinct vision of God and how it relates to their lives. This vision frames the context for worship practices, preaching, and the cultivation of faith in the lives of the people. Redeeming Life believes that God cares about matters of the spirit like prayer, worship, and reading Scripture. Material matters like finances, jobs, cars, schools and where you live are just as important. God cares about every facet of your life, especially the existential plight of people in the southern West Virginia region. God cares about people who can't pay their bills. God cares about people who cannot afford health insurance. God cares about how humiliating it feels to stand in line to apply for food stamps because you cannot afford to feed your own family. God cares about people who walk to work or the store while people drive by in cars.

There are actually two particular theological streams of influence that converge in unique ways in prosperity churches: the existential focus in traditional black church thought and the Pentecostal emphasis on pneumatological immanence. This belief represents a redefining or amending of a traditional belief or core emphasis in black church thinking, which is a focus on existential or lived issues. Faith or theology in the black church invariably begins with existential or lived experience. This emphasis is seen most clearly in black preaching. Some of the most powerful sermons in the history of the black church focus on existential issues or dilemmas. This preaching tradition continues in prosperity churches. In sermons, the pastor is careful to connect human need with the God who created them and cares for them. Often biblical stories like Hannah's prayer for a son in 1 Samuel, the widow of Zarephath in 1 Kings, or the woman with the flow of blood in Mark are used to illustrate God's concern for desperate human need and acute suffering. People in West Virginia have their life stories framed through the lens of those in Scripture who know what it is like to be in difficult situations. The difference between these neo-Charismatics and more traditional Baptists and Pentecostals is the belief that divine presence, once encountered in worship and active faith, means one's life can change. Why the difference? Because for them it is important that people know they can do something about their plight. This is why the pastor insists that things can get better in our lives. He fundamentally rejects a theology that assigns people to poverty and mediocrity. Christians, or "believers" as the pastor called them, should expect to see blessings because this is a natural result of the concern God has for his children. God wants better for them to and will work alongside them to make changes.

How does one make a difference in his or her life? It begins by encountering God in worship. The experience of divine presence during praise and worship is significant, taking up as much time in the worship service as preaching. If one has not encountered and been touched by God he or she has not really worshiped God. This is a Pentecostal belief and religious practice that has undergone change with the proliferation of Charismatic and nondenominational churches. The encounter with the presence of God happens while worshiping, during praise and worship, not necessarily at the altar after the sermon, which is a practice in black denominational Pentecostal churches. During this time there is a divine-human exchange. Praise leaders give parishioners space to pour our hearts out to God and to receive ministry from God. In worship they expect God to touch and strengthen them. There are a wide array of practices employed by people during praise and worship: people stand to reverence God, raise their hands, dance, walk around, sing, pray in tongues, weep, and bow. There are times when the pastor or one of the elders sense that people may need special prayer and they are invited to the altar for prayer and a prophetic word. This can happen before or after the message. Both the vision of God put before the people and the communal experience of divine presence provides the ground for new possibilities in life.

Change occurs when believers act on their faith. African American faith teachers like Fred Brown, who studied at Rhema, maintain that faith is essential to change. But their understanding of faith is different than what traditional Baptist and Pentecostal pastors believe. These hybrid Pentecostals are not thinking about "the faith" as in the body of Christian beliefs or the "faith in God" of one who believes in the saving or redemptive work of God for the world. For these teachers, faith is what activates and makes operative in a person's life, all that they believe God can and will do. Brown studied under Hagin at Rhema but was heavily influenced by Price, and was affiliated with his network the Fellowship of Inner City Word of Faith Ministries, while I was a member. So I will briefly summarize Price's understanding of faith before discussing Brown's teachings at Redeeming Life. In the book *How Faith Works*, Fred Price referred to faith as the activator of all other aspects of the Christian's life and that "everything in the kingdom is activated and accessed by faith."[5] Both spiritual disciplines and gifts like love, obedience, and prayer are all rightly operated by faith. So for him, faith touches all aspects of one's life. He also contends that faith and belief are different. Belief does not act; it only assents to the validity or truthfulness of a conviction. Belief, while good and even necessary, is not as important as faith because "it will not change your circumstances or bring results."[6] Faith acts on what is believed instead of passively assenting to a belief. A Christian can believe God can heal, but that is mere passive assent, whereas having or exercising faith that God will heal is qualitatively different. One can believe God can provide, but never experience provision in his or her life until he or she acts on this belief. This is a significant point. Change is not possible unless one acts in faith. By acting on what you believe, the promises of God can become a reality in one's life. And for Price faith works in all contexts and for all people because faith is "the active dynamic power activator which releases the power of Almighty God in your life and circumstances."[7]

These teachings took on a different form in West Virginia. Brown stressed faith but did so by framing a believer's life as a story of faith with both ups and downs, but through it all experiences of the faithfulness of God. One of his favorite scriptures was Romans 1:17, "The righteousness of God is revealed from faith to faith." This text accents the unfolding nature of the life of faith and was apropos for people whose lives were

---

5. Price, *How Faith Works*, 11.
6. Ibid., 18.
7. Price, *Now Faith Is Substance Evidence Hebrews 11:1*, 6.

far from a finished product. The text he most often utilized to illustrate this was the story of the children of Israel in the Old Testament books of Exodus, Numbers, and Joshua. These books documents their story from slavery in Egypt to freedom, independence, and blessing in the land of promise. This story, which begins with a promise to Abraham in Genesis 12, functions as an overarching theme in his preaching. Whole sermon series were based on this story and frequent allusions to it were made. In one's life there is a trajectory from a life of difficulty or mediocrity before encountering God to a life of blessing and prosperity. This journey begins with salvation and being filled with the Holy Spirit but it is not just salvific. God wants to do more than save souls and fill them with the power of the Spirit. God desires that they experience abundant life, a promise recorded in the Gospel of John. This means that the life of faith is a process that unfolds itself over time as we respond in faith to God and that areas of our lives such as our marriages, families, and finances should get better.

Where does one begin after salvation? For Brown, people begin where they are. He emphasized the importance of individual initiative and responsibility. Because jobs were scarce and poverty was so widespread, there was a tendency among some blacks to resign themselves to a life of poverty and mediocrity. Some would not try to do better. They would not look for a job or accept a minimum wage job or even a temporary job. They would sit around and do nothing while yet expecting their life to change. Brown would not accept such reasoning and challenged it on numerous occasions. We had to do something and begin with what little we had. Two texts were instrumental in reinforcing this message: the parable of the mustard seed in Matthew and the story of Moses's call to return to Egypt. One sermon emphasized the importance of utilizing "what's in your hand" to be the key to your miracle and provision. For Brown, God starts where you are and with what you have. That is why it was important that in faith we put our best foot forward. This consisted of simple acts like applying for another job or taking a low-paying job to make ends meet. It could be taking two jobs for now, or going back to school while working full time. That might be where you start, but if that act is done in faith that God has better for you, some opportunity will come. Not doing so was actually an act of unfaithfulness rooted in beliefs that God could do nothing to change our situation. Brown preached that such responses were rooted in "stinking thinking." He emphasized this in a sermon on Numbers 13, where the spies returned to Moses with an evil report. Ten of the spies perceived they could not defeat the "giants" in the land and so encouraged a large contingency of people to appoint another leader and return to Egypt. This was illustrative of an attitude Brown thought was counterproductive. An "I can't" or "we can't" attitude could nullify what God may want to do and, there was no room for stinking thinking at Redeeming Life, because we, like Joshua and Caleb in Numbers 13, believed we could possess the promises of God.

Pastor Brown did not just expect people to try. Faith doesn't just "wing it," but instead takes actions that reflect an attitude of expectancy. I remember him saying, "The atmosphere of expectancy is the breeding ground for miracles." If one expected God to change his or her life then believers were committed to doing their best work in preparation for God's blessing. Brown emphasized this in three ways: by his insistence on excellence in life and ministry, by "prosperity connections," and by stressing the importance of vision (what you see by faith). During my time at Redeeming Life one of our emphases was that we were committed to being a church of excellence. Everything we set out to do was to be done in a spirit of excellence. This insistence came directly from the pastor, who strove for excellence in all areas of life. Excellence was demonstrated in a variety of ways: keeping the church clean and looking immaculate, doing good work when asked, going above what is expected or what people consider average or enough, and being organized in ministry and life tasks. In a culture that tempts people to accept mediocrity, excellence was our standard because it best reflected the God we represented. Prosperity connections is a different way of talking about communalism and good relationships. If you want to succeed in life then you need to associate with people who are going somewhere. Pastor Brown made sure we were exposed to a steady dose of successful and ambitious leaders in ministry and business who were willing to pass on what they knew. These people would travel from Washington DC, Baltimore, Charlotte, and Tulsa to Bluefield. For some people this was the first time they met a highly successful black person. Brown exposed us to these people because he believed prosperity is dependent upon the people around you. People can either increase your capacity to prosper or decrease it. Furthermore, he took his calling very seriously because he believed our lives should be enriched by our association with him.

Vision was absolutely essential to a life of prosperity. Often we would hear him quote the text out of Proverbs, "Where there is no vision, people perish." One of the primary roles of his preaching was to instill a vision of better things and higher expectations in the minds of the people. He worked hard to insure that his people did not succumb to a "poverty mentality" that did not expect better in life. Stories and illustrations suffused his sermons. Sometimes he would use props, and always humor. But people could not catch the vision without seeing things differently themselves. That is why the pastor thought it was important for people in this region to travel and see a different side of the world. He wanted them to see that there was a different side of life and that life was possible for them. It was important for people to see that everybody in the world is not struggling and sad. So he found ways to expose the members of the church to the other side of life that he preached about in sermons. He would host conferences in places like Charlotte in a nice hotel. On one occasion the church sponsored a trip to the Bahamas and took a large contingency of people outside the country for the first time. Doing this was a part of changing the mentality of the people and opening their minds to new possibilities. While people worked hard to come up with money for trips like this, even sacrificing money for other important and essential things, for many it was an investment in a better life. Pastor Brown knew this and used the institutional power and finances of the church to leverage opportunities for people, some of whom were not even members of our church. Even smaller things like fishing trips to the ocean or eating at a nice restaurant were ways to sow seeds in the minds and lives of poor and disenfranchised people. Sitting in nice conference rooms or driving onto the grounds of a resort and being treated like a person of worth had a powerful effect on one's confidence and sense of self. The commitment to excellence, positive associations, and a vision of a better life instills a sense of determination and focus to see the process and journey through, whether that means going back to school or transitioning to a new profession.

There was an attempt to balance individual initiative and responsibility and the communal support necessary to live into the blessings of God. Brown stressed individualism because initiative, effort, and responsibility are important. But he realized that success does not just come about because one works hard. Room is made in his theology for difficulties in life that require the help of others. He understood that there were larger forces at work trying to keep you and all the people he ministered to locked in a box of lack, frustration, despair, and bitterness. And this lifestyle is a vicious cycle that repeats itself for generations. With the language of New Testament texts like Ephesians 6:12 and 2 Corinthians 4:3,

Brown focused on the spiritual root or cause for this and spoke of it often in his messages. Satan was the god of this world and worked through his host of demons to thwart the righteous and keep them living a life of sickness, suffering, and misery. Brown used the language of spiritual attacks and trials of faith. Satan and demons are evil spirits and humans and human institutions carry out their work. So there is a dual source to the trouble that believers encounter: human and demonic. He does not blame everything evil on the devil, nor does he humanize all evil and suffering. It is both. And both, he believes, are the reasons there is so much depression, unemployment, violence, hopelessness, and poverty in the region.

Communal support is an overlooked part of the prosperity theology system. Many believe that it is a theology that hinges solely on individualism. That is incorrect. Teachers like Brown emphasize both. The whole point of prosperity is the realization of the promise God gave to Abraham. God desires to bless you individually so you can bless others. Why? Because need is so great in the world. The point of preaching prosperity amidst poverty and hopelessness is to change these devastating conditions. The goal is to cause a reversal of cycles—from a cycle of lack to a cycle of abundance. This was the vision that the members of Redeeming Life were invited to participate in. We were enlisted and called by God to reverse cycles of miseducation, unemployment, and poverty and to help others live into this holistic communal vision.

This requires a balance of individual initiative and communal support, a balance that is not easily nor perfectly maintained. But there was a sincere effort to balance both. On one hand each person was expected to do his or her best and grow. After all, how can you help someone if you are always struggling? Brown preached a message entitled "The Greed of Need," which spoke about those who are perpetually in a state of need and do not seek to improve their lives. He used the illustration of the person who sits at home saying he is waiting on God to send a job his way. There is something wrong when we just grovel in need and don't try to do better, mostly because it means someone else is footing the bill for you. Someone is paying the rent while you sit and wait on God. On the other hand, we were taught and encouraged to be generous and not to take all we can for ourselves. Two notable examples of this are that people would pay for others to travel and also would lend money and vehicles to people in need. In fact, middle-class blacks had a distinct role or ministry in this church. They served as a valuable model of what's possible. The fact that they could prosper in this depressed region was a testimony, a witness of what was possible. Occasionally they would testify about their blessings during worship to inspire others to keep the faith and give. These members were also an invaluable support for the church. They were major givers to the church. They would bless and encourage less fortunate blacks with food, clothing, assistance for going on trips, and rides to church and the store. Less fortunate blacks needed two things from people who had prospered to a greater extent: aid negotiating the challenges of poverty and, more importantly, a model, an example or path of how to get out of the vicious cycle themselves. This communalism was essential for one to escape the prison of poverty.

The last component of his message was the essential nature of giving. Brown could not see how God could bless a person who is not faithful with their finances. Believers must steward what they have if they expect God to entrust more to them. Like many Christian pastors and churches, not just those who teach prosperity, he stressed the importance of giving both tithes and offerings. A tithe is giving 10 percent of your gross income, and offerings were financial gifts over and above the tithe. If a person worked a job and made $10 per hour and worked forty hours per week, her gross pay would be $400. The government would deduct its percentage for federal and state taxes, and there may have been other deductions for things like health insurance. While one's take home pay may have been $320 or $330, their tithe to the church would be $40, and they would also be expected to give an offering, sometimes two offerings. Sample Scriptures used to regulate this practice were Leviticus 27:32, Malachi 3:8–10, Luke 6:38, and 2 Corinthians 9. Giving is a command that is binding on all Christians, and when a person disobeys this command he unleashes a curse that primarily manifests itself in their finances. His line of thinking is greatly informed by reading texts like Deuteronomy 28 and Malachi 3. These texts seem to suggest that cursing is the result of disobedience of covenant commands. And it did not matter what a person's income was—the command to tithe and give offerings was binding.

Giving was so important to his ministry that it occupied a part of the service. After praise and worship, Pastor Brown or one of the ministers of the church would teach on giving for a few minutes before receiving tithes and offerings. And sometimes the tithe would be given first and then the offering. This part was not rushed through; great care was taken to teach what the Bible says about giving and what happens in a believer's life when they are faithful to God's command. Why give so much attention to giving? The answer is more contextual than doctrinal. Money was a taboo issue for many in the region. Money was shrouded in a cloud of ignorance and fear. The offering is usually a very uncomfortable time in worship for many churches in this region, and not just because there is so much poverty. Many denominational pastors thought it was wrong to talk about money over the pulpit. But Brown and the church were not shy about the issue of money. They talked about money because it was an issue of faith, along with salvation, forgiveness, holiness, and prayer. The emphasis on money was actually challenging the prevailing ethos of ignorance. When teaching on giving, Brown would often correct beliefs that seemed to contradict the Bible's teachings and any notion that a person can be blessed while not giving to the things of God. For example, he frequently criticized the popular opinion that "all the church wants is your money." Beyond what the Bible teaches, he reminded us that everything in the world operates by money. Businesses, schools, and even places of entertainment all require money to sustain themselves. Why is ministry any different? He said, "Prayer does not pay light bills and faith does not pay the mortgage. Money does." He taught that everybody wants your money because that is how the world works. To him, this critique is utter foolishness because it assumes the church does not operate like other businesses. Challenging the critiques against giving in the church was essential because there was so much opposition to this teaching among the denominational churches. For Brown, making money a taboo issue only insured that poor and middle-class blacks were ignorant about it and, more importantly, about how the world works. Money and other business and economic issues are at the core of how the world works and they needed to know this.

So the question is, "Why did he hold to such a standard and belief?" Brown's theology of giving is rooted in the belief that it makes a difference in one's individual life and the life of the church. Brown would make a radical statement. He believed that a person could give her way out of poverty. There is both a spiritual and practical component to this teaching. First, his theology reflects a belief that God is a partner in blessing his people and that giving is an avenue of divine blessing. One cannot get out of the cycle of poverty by holding on to the little he has; instead, he needs to see what he has as a resource or seed God can use to do more in his life. This is a different way to think about what you have, even if it is less than what you would like to have. Brown did not want people thinking they had nothing or could do nothing for themselves. Even if it is only ten extra dollars a week, you can use that to change your situation for the better. He often used the language of seed to talk about this process. While the seed looks insignificant, it yields a harvest, which is why he challenged us not to eat our seed. That is a life practice that yields zero results and keeps people locked in a bad situation. Second, giving teaches important practical life principles that yield blessings: budgeting, living within one's means, delayed gratification, and sacrifice. These are not the worst lessons one could learn about finances.

Many believed that the pastor was receiving all the money. That was not true. We supported our pastor financially, but his emphasis on giving was not to increase his salary. If he wanted to make a lot of money I am sure he could have done so pastoring churches in other places besides southern West Virginia. We believed that there was nothing wrong with blessing our pastor and supporting his family. He lived in a nice home and drove nice cars, but was not living in the largest home in town. He was no millionaire, though he would not object to being one. He was blessed and prosperous. And his source of blessing was not coming from the offerings of poor people in West Virginia. He was a tentmaker of sorts. He preached all over the country in churches of all denominations, both to preach the gospel to the world and to support his family because the church could not offer an adequate salary for him. Giving was not about what he could get from the people. I believe the main reason he held such a high standard of giving was because giving results in good being done in the larger community. When members give to the church, it enables the church to continue doing good. Without members giving, ministry is not possible. His emphases on giving and money are so strong because ministry is being done and it is making a difference in the lives of many.

The message and ministry of Fred Brown and Redeeming Life Christian Center provide a compelling case study of what it means to do ministry in the black community in the late twentieth century. He sought to lay before people a radical vision of a God who cares and is invested in changing things in their lives for the better. He rejected any belief that blacks were stuck in a system that they could not get out of. He firmly believed that they could do something about their situation. He rejected any narrative of victimization. Blacks could go from unemployed and poor to employed and prosperous. The church was invested in living out this vision together with them.

It is an absurdity to suggest this movement and message is exclusively about money or being a millionaire. It is not exclusively individualistic. Instead, it is a message that gives meaning and hope to people who are marginalized, yet want a better life. Does it work? Yes. My life has been blessed and enriched by being a part of this church and its network of churches and ministries for the past seventeen years. It has worked for many people who attend this church and now pastor churches and work better jobs than they did in the late nineties. Does it work for every person in every situation? No. But no theological system or church doctrine or ministry works for all people and in all situations. It gives meaning and hope and is communal, the stuff of good theology and community. I believe this movement will be relevant for years to come because it holds the promise of better for poor and middle-class blacks in West Virginia and millions of blacks across this country who struggle against poverty and marginalization. I suspect a major reason for memberships and attendance in these churches is the hard social realities confronting black Americans.

The message and ministry of Fred Brown and the Redeeming Life Church in a small town in West Virginia provide the seeds of a larger Pentecostal theology of the poor that Pentecostalism and the traditions of the black church have yet to develop. Instead, they rely on white mainline and evangelical theologies to speak to the experience of marginalization, to judge indigenous and contextual theologies, and sometimes these theologies ignore the poor and marginalized altogether. Surely there has to be a better way to begin construction of a Pentecostal theology that speaks to the experience of poverty and marginalization.

I think this theology begins by not making poor blacks and Pentecostals the objects of study, but instead participants in thriving communities with theologies worthy of engagement, appreciation, and criticism. Greater attention needs to be given to their voices and the ways they construct meaning amidst oppressing and despairing conditions. What we will find is that poor and marginalized communities have gifts of perspective, insight, and practice that can illumine the broader task of theology. It is time to give greater attention to local and nonpopular theological voices as churches grapple with issues of local, regional, national, and global poverty and the plethora of ways they impact people's lives. They don't need us to do theology for them. They need us to do theology with them.

We have a beginning point in this chapter because I began not with the assumption that it is my place to judge the theology of others by popular or academic mainline or evangelical theological categories, but by trying to ascertain the nature and function of a theology in a poor context. This attempt to suspend judgment and not rely on prescribed theological categories—prosperity is a new form of New Thought metaphysics, prosperity is a new form of Christian Science, prosperity is a new form of Christian capitalism, etc.—allowed me to explore how prosperity theology could actually benefit a poor community instead of exploiting it. We also have a beginning point because I believe that it is not the task of theology to speak for all people, but to discern the contours and shape of theology in its varied contexts. I wanted to discern not so much a prosperity theology as if it were a single thing, but rather to discern one of the theological streams of this movement in the context of West Virginia.

CONCLUSION

It is good news when a prosperity teacher shares a message that God cares about the poor and marginalized, God can change their situation, God's work provides the ground for an alternative life, and committing one's life to God, in faith, can lead to progress and change. In other words, in the face of difficult and sometimes hopeless situations, black prosperity teachers contend that the future can be better and people have a large measure of control as to whether that happens. This is not to say that people experience results all the time, because they do not. But the message resonates with their need and hope for a better life because it is rooted in a theology that insists God cares about the experience of poverty and marginalization. To that end, it is good news. While there is much to criticize about this movement, especially at the popular level, there is more to this movement than what scholars and popular pastors critique. There are positive dimensions of this movement and its teachings, especially in poor communities, and I hope scholars will turn their attention to some of these streams as this movement is studied in the future.

— CHAPTER 5 —

Is Prosperity Teaching the New Pentecostal Message?

THE PHENOMENAL GROWTH OF the Pentecostal movement across the world is one of the most significant developments in the field of religion. Vinson Synan, a prominent Pentecostal historian, gives convincing evidence for this in the book *In the Latter Days*. He says that many of the largest congregations and denominations are those affiliated with Pentecostalism, that the five most sizable congregations in the world are Pentecostal of some kind, and that the leading figures of the electronic church, often referred to as televangelists, and the largest evangelistic crusades held in the world are all linked to Pentecostalism.[1] Pentecostals have been the leading innovators in congregational, media, and evangelistic ministry and continue to impact the religious world in a myriad of ways. Though often ignored by many religious scholars, Pentecostalism is one of the most significant movements in global Christianity and global religion.

The prosperity movement is one of, if not the most significant developments in Pentecostalism in the past three decades. For example, Canaanland, also referred to as Winner's Chapel, is a nondenominational church in Lagos, Nigeria. David Oyedepo, the pastor of this church with a weekly attendance of over 50,000 people, preaches prosperity along with a number of very large nondenominational churches spread across

---

1. Synan, *In the Latter Days*, 22–24.

the continent. David Cho, pastor of the largest church in the world, and Joel Osteen, pastor the largest church in the United States, both preach prosperity. The influence of this movement is widespread. While not all Pentecostal churches have embraced prosperity teaching, a large number of these churches do teach varying forms of prosperity in their churches and promote it in their denominations and/or networks of nondenominational churches.

It is difficult to ascertain the extent of the impact this movement has had on global Pentecostalism and whether the prosperity movement is still growing in influence, especially considering the large number of hybrid or neo-Charismatic nondenominational churches. These churches are quasi-Pentecostal. The widespread influence of this movement raises a host of questions about the future of global Pentecostalism. Will the message of prosperity continue to resonate with people in Pentecostal, Charismatic, and neo-Charismatic churches? Will it change the narrative of global Pentecostalism? Is the future of Pentecostalism inextricably linked to this message? Is prosperity the new Pentecostal message? The answers to such questions are complex, and only time will tell if this doctrine becomes one of the central teachings of Pentecostals, but Pentecostals need to have a conversation about the influence of this movement, its message, and its implication for the future of Pentecostalism. And the conversation needs to involve practitioners of prosperity teaching, critics of the movement, and the growing cadre of scholars and historians of Pentecostalism. All have a vested interest in the conversation about the future of Pentecostalism. I offer this chapter as a primer that will hopefully facilitate this much-needed dialogue.

The message of prosperity will continue to influence the global Pentecostal movement. The various manifestations of prosperity teaching are extensions of Pentecostal beliefs about God and the implications of divine presence on human living. Pentecostals believe that there is more to Christian living than salvation and church attendance. There are other blessings that are essential: sanctification and Spirit baptism are two examples. For Pentecostals, God also meets human need. One of the core doctrines of early Pentecostalism was divine healing, and this doctrine remains a vital part of Pentecostal teaching. Pentecostals believe that Jesus is a healer. Healing was a large part of the ministry of Jesus in the Gospels, and Pentecostals see themselves as participating in that ministry. This is why healing has been a central doctrine of Pentecostalism throughout the twentieth century. If people can experience God's presence in a way that leads to a baptism of the Holy Spirit, and if they can experience bodily healing in response to believing prayer, then it is not a stretch to extend this belief to prospering in one's life. It is not a stretch to claim that God wants to bless persons and meet all their needs. It is just an extension of beliefs about Spirit baptism and healing. This message will continue to resonate with people in the Pentecostal movement because it is a reformulation of Pentecostal doctrines. A clear example of this is the Word of Faith movement. Word of Faith teaching appropriated aspects of New Thought metaphysics, Mind Science, and secular beliefs from a capitalistic society, but the theological core was Pentecostal. This core is one reason denominational Pentecostals adopted aspects of the prosperity doctrine, such as the belief that God will meet believers' financial needs.

Prosperity teaching continues in spite of two decades of criticism. Exposing the influence of New Thought and Mind Science and the critique that the teaching is heretical resulted in a process of amending these beliefs. Some prosperity teachers have retreated from radical forms to more Pentecostal beliefs. Jim Bakker is an example. Once a major proponent of prosperity teaching, he rejected it and embraced the apocalyptic beliefs of early Pentecostalism, namely the imminent return of Jesus Christ. The critiques levied by scholars and the scandals involving popular advocates of the message have caused some pastors to amend some of the radical forms of this teaching, particularly the heavy emphasis on positive confession, as if words can materialize money, and the expectation that God wants every Christian to be a millionaire. The "name it and claim it" and "money cometh" brands of prosperity have lost favor in recent years, while the more pragmatic forms of prosperity preached by Jakes, Dollar, and Osteen have persisted. God wants you to be happy. God wants you to be your best. God wants you to fulfill your purpose. God wants your needs to be met. God wants to bless you so you can bless others. God wants you to live a life free from debt. This message continues after the economic collapse of 2008 and I suspect it will continue for years to come. It will be especially important to pay attention to the many changes these teachings undergo as beliefs are amended in light of decades of heavy criticism. It is possible that new or amended forms of prosperity teaching will emerge in the coming years.

If prosperity teaching continues to be popular and if forms of its teaching change, will this result in prosperity becoming the central or new Pentecostal message? I would not go so far as to say that prosperity is the new Pentecostal message, but millions of people who are a part of the movement may say otherwise. For them, this message may be the new Pentecostal theme, whether critics and scholars like it or not. In spite of prosperity teachers' participation and belief in the Pentecostal message, I am not sure if this would be good for the movement. This is a complex issue that will require further discussion.

WHY PROSPERITY GOSPEL COULD BE THE NEW PENTECOSTAL MESSAGE

There is cause for optimism if an amended form or forms of prosperity teaching becomes the new Pentecostal message. I say this because of two developments within Pentecostalism. In their book *Pentecostalism and the Future of the Christian Churches*, Richard Schaull and Waldo Cesar shared an important insight about Pentecostalism outside the United States. They found that Pentecostalism is strongest in the poorest parts of the world and that there is something they find in Pentecostalism that helps the poorest of the poor to find meaning and hope. They cited David Barrett's statistic that half of all Pentecostals, approximately 200 million persons, live in shantytowns in the depths of poverty, and that nineteen million represent the poorest of the poor, who have to scrape through the rubbish heaps each day in search of food.[2] The growth of Pentecostalism among the poor has led scholars such as Schaull and Cesar to refer to Pentecostalism in Africa, Asia, and South America as the church of the poor. I believe that what makes Pentecostalism so vibrant among the poor is that it gives them a place to exercise their agency as people of God and it does not merely treat them as victims of an oppressive global economy. Pentecostals who are poor serve as pastors, bishops, worship leaders, and hold other leadership positions in church. They receive dreams and visions and operate in the gifts of the Spirit. They encounter and experience a God who does not show favoritism. In church, they are sons and daughters of God, ambassadors of the kingdom of heaven, prophets and prophetesses, teachers and healers who are called to the world. Furthermore, these Pentecostals lead churches and networks of ministries. In Pentecostalism, a leader can be financially poor but spiritually gifted and proven to be a valuable leader in church and the community. The choice

2. Schaull and Cesar, *Pentecostalism and the Future of the Christian Churches*, 126–27.

of the poor to turn to Pentecostalism in their quest for meaning and hope is a significant development and a sign of great hope.

The second development is the emergence of progressive Pentecostalism. Progressive Pentecostalism describes a type of Pentecostalism that is gaining momentum in Africa, Asia, and South America. "Pentecostalism has often been otherworldly, emphasizing personal salvation to the exclusion of any attempt to transform social reality."[3] So this term describes an emerging group of Pentecostals who affirms "the apocalyptic return of Christ but also [believe] that Christians are called to be good neighbors, addressing the social needs of the people in their community."[4] These Pentecostals address the AIDS pandemic in Africa, educate children, and meet the needs of the impoverished while retaining the vibrant spirituality that characterizes Pentecostalism. Donald Miller and Tetsuano Yamamori excluded both the Pentecostals who identify with the right-wing repressive governments (like the religious Right in America) and Pentecostals who focus exclusively on health and wealth teaching. This is at least an indirect criticism of American Pentecostalism. The Pentecostalism that is so popular among the poor and that takes social ministry seriously is qualitatively different than the kind broadcasted on television in America. But my question is, what if there were healthy expressions of prosperity teaching that aligned themselves with progressive Pentecostals? This could be an expression of teaching with not only great appeal but also relevance for the needs of the poor.

The only chance that prosperity teaching has in becoming the new Pentecostal message is if it addresses issues of global poverty and the manifold ways they impact the lives of the poorest of the poor. The prosperity gospel is thriving in the poorest parts of the world because many Pentecostals in these countries are poor. Pentecostal pastors of varied kinds are present in poor communities and preach a message that refuses to victimize the poor but instead tells them they can do something about their situation. Some brands of prosperity preaching can be good news to the poor because they are guided by the belief that God cares about the spiritual and material well-being of all humans; that salvation has both spiritual and socioeconomic implications; and finally, that one can expect and seek blessings from God, who desires to bless his people. In some

---

3. Miller and Yamamori, *Global Pentecostalism*, 2.
4. Ibid.

respects, this could be the new Pentecostal message because Pentecostalism thrives in countries where there is extreme poverty.

Prosperity teaching holds promise for Pentecostals who are the poorest of the poor because the message may speak to millions and possibly billions living in poverty. There is so much poverty in the world that this movement and its message will resonate with many for the foreseeable future. Poor people may find promise in the movement, whether scholars like the theology or not. And they may continue to be drawn to the message and its churches because in it they hear that God cares about their material conditions and needs, that God cares about the poor and marginalized, and that God wants better for the poor. This can be good news. If this form of prosperity teaching continues and if poor and marginalized communities find a word of hope in this message as they define themselves and use their agency to find hope amidst the hopeless conditions they face, then this could be the new Pentecostal message. There is potential that an amended form or forms of prosperity teaching could become a core message of Pentecostalism. On the other hand, if this occurs it would pose some dangers.

WHY PROSPERITY SHOULD NOT BE THE NEW PENTECOSTAL MESSAGE

First, I am concerned because it would represent a definitive shift in the movement from the centrality of the Holy Spirit. Pentecostalism became prominent because of its focus on sanctification, the baptism of the Spirit, speaking in tongues, healing, deliverance, and the second coming. The ministry of the Holy Spirit was clearly central for Pentecostals. People were invited to be baptized in the Spirit, to be filled with the Spirit, to be anointed by the Spirit for ministry, and to encounter the power and presence of the Spirit in worship services. This encounter led to healing, deliverance, and a stronger relationship with God. The experience and anointing of the Spirit made the difference in one's life and was preached on and sought by many for almost a century. This emphasis has gradually changed.

In the last decade of the twentieth century and first decade of the twenty-first century, the message of Pentecostalism no longer centralizes the Spirit but rather human success and achievement. The prosperity emphasis has eclipsed the insistence on holiness, Spirit baptism, tongues, and the anointing. American Pentecostalism is increasingly giving itself over to the appearance and love of success with the proliferation of megachurches, television ministries, and celebrity preachers. There are also major conferences that showcase preachers and singers who put on events that rival secular concerts in entertainment value. Much of this operates under the façade of success and the belief that churches grow because their pastors are successful, accomplished, and effective leaders. Successful ministries can afford to have a television ministry and sponsor major conferences. Success is quietly becoming a dominant part of the message of American Pentecostalism. And this message is promoted globally. American missionaries, major pastors, and televangelists have made a major impact on Pentecostalism in South America, Africa, and parts of Asia with the message of prosperity.

The result has been a decentralization of the importance of the Spirit, which, to me, is at the heart of what it means to be Pentecostal. In today's Pentecostal church, one is more likely to hear a message about success, blessings, and prosperity than to hear a message about the Holy Spirit. In today's Pentecostal church, people do not necessarily need the Holy Ghost anymore; rather, they need blessings. This is what is emphasized as central and is clearly a major shift in the movement. It has resulted in an increasing sense of confusion among Pentecostals about what makes one Pentecostal. Pentecostal identity used to center around the work of the Spirit in the life of the church and community. Now, it is quite possible that what identifies Pentecostalism is success.

This is only the tip of the iceberg. The growing message of prosperity, in addition to other developments, is a sign that Pentecostalism is two decades into an identity crisis. For example, in the nineties an increasing number of Pentecostals aligned themselves with the religious Right and the culture (not the religion) of conservative evangelicalism. Worse yet, now there are Tea Party Pentecostals marching around with those invested in taking their country back from minorities, immigrants, and the poor. With these very conservative Christians filling pulpits and pews in Pentecostal churches, beside middle-class and more and more wealthy white Christians, there is less talk about the Spirit, no talk about social justice, and more focus on using the Bible, religion, and the government to protect their interests and privileges. It appears that Pentecostalism is increasingly losing its prophetic edge.

The message of prosperity is a small part of a much larger shift in the Pentecostal movement that is jeopardizing its prophetic edge and relevance for global Christianity. Aligning Pentecostalism with privilege and the interests of the wealthy few instead of viewing itself as a movement for the billions of marginalized people in the world is a major mistake and a discouraging sign for the future of Pentecostalism. Pentecostals are not talking about the Holy Spirit very much these days. Instead the focus is on blessings, success, and one's place within the American empire—who deserves to get the most and why they deserve it. As long as prosperity teaching continues to decentralize the ministry of the Spirit and instead centralizes a social vision of success that is limited to wealthy, privileged persons, it should not be considered the new Pentecostal message.

Second, prosperity teaching should not be the new Pentecostal message because, though it can possibly offer hope to the poor and oppressed, the theology that undergirds the message is still underdeveloped and does not look at issues from a systemic standpoint. With a few exceptions, prosperity teaching is primarily individualistic. This is a glaring oversight. The agency of the individual is affirmed and possibilities encouraged, but there is not an emphasis on the communal well-being or any critique of society. It is significant that Pentecostalism resonates with the poorest of the poor, but that is not enough. Pentecostals need to take an additional step, especially advocates of the prosperity message. A good place to begin is with a question: "Why is there the kind of poverty that leaves 200 million people living in shantytowns and digging through trash heaps for food?" In other words, prosperity teachers have to take up issues of systemic poverty and not individualize poverty, gloss over, or hide from the hard realities of poverty under the language of generational curses, divine favor, and the like. Teachers have to take another step beyond what happens when an individual believes and acts in faith to a fuller account of the social obstacles that affect the people of God.

The next step for prosperity teaching is twofold. It first involves addressing poverty systemically. For example, teachers of prosperity have to connect the poverty that Pentecostals experience with the poverty experienced by millions of other people. I have serious doubts that prosperity teachers are willing or able to do this, primarily because American Pentecostalism is still slow in developing theologies that address issues from a systemic standpoint. Given the widespread impact of the American brand of Pentecostalism on prosperity preaching churches in the majority world, I suspect that they too may be unable and unwilling to look at poverty in this manner. Issues of poverty are spiritualized with beliefs that poverty is a curse or the devil wants believers to be poor. These beliefs can be helpful but are limited when ignoring what humans do with the institutions and resources of this world. Prosperity teachers have to address systemic poverty in their preaching and teaching. They have to see poverty in their churches and communities as a part of a larger system of poverty affecting billions of people. And this kind of poverty has nothing to do with individual sin or a lack of faith. It is the way the world has been ordered by generations of select families and individuals with wealth, religious and political power, and privilege.

Today, billions of people are born into a world where an estimated 2.8 billion people, nearly half of the world's population, survive on less than $2 per day. And one-fifth of the world's population (1.2 billion) survive on less than $1 per day. More than 3 billion people are chronically hungry and live in absolute poverty.[5] The human toll of poverty that is so widespread is significant. For example, more people have died from hunger in the past five years than have been killed in all the wars, revolutions, and murders in the past 150 years.[6] Pentecostal and prosperity teachers cannot turn a blind eye to the real workings of the global economy. Prosperity teachers have to probe the social world as much as the spiritual one when trying to understand why there is poverty. Until prosperity teaching takes up such issues, it should not be the new Pentecostal message.

Not only must Pentecostals address the horrible realities of systemic poverty, they have to do so against the backdrop of a widening wealth gap. This is the second part of the next step that prosperity teaching needs to take. It has to take more earnestly its calling to critique this system. While the poor suffer today, the rich are getting richer. Elizabeth Hinson-Hasty, a Presbyterian theologian, argues that the problem of wealth is "the most pressing theological and moral problem of our time."[7] The widening wealth gap in the US and around the world is alarming and has significant implications for the lives of billions of citizens of the world and the church. Some examples follow.

- There were 1,645 billionaires globally as of March 2014, according to Forbes data cited in the Oxfam report, up from 793 in March 2009.
- The world's richest 85 people's collective wealth is equal to the wealth of the poorest half of the world's population.

---

5. Winter and Hawthorne, *Perspectives on World Christian Movement*, 569–70.
6. Trull, *Walking in the Way*, 263.
7. Hinson-Hasty, "The Problem of Wealth," 39.

- The richest 10 percent owns 85 percent of global wealth. The bottom half of the world's population possesses barely 1 percent of total global wealth.[8]

Wealth accumulation is one problem, but the inequitable distribution of wealth is a different kind of problem with which the church must contend.[9] Hinson-Hasty showed that faith leaders respond to the problem of wealth by accommodating their beliefs to the culture, particularly capitalism. There are some prosperity teachers who have done this. Worse yet, some ministries function like businesses whose sole purpose is to create wealth for the chief officer. Prosperity teachers in America are comfortable with the language and culture of capitalism, which is one reason for the critiques of this form of teaching. For religious scholars like Hinson-Hasty, this is a form of idolatry. Her work is important because it forces movements like the American prosperity movement to address the extent of their participation in the idolatry of the market. There are forms of prosperity teaching that participate in idolatry and until these things are addressed, prosperity should not be the new Pentecostal message.

Hinson-Hasty's work provides an additional benefit. She invites faith communities to take a critical look at the machinations of the market and to attempt to discern the extent of participation in both injustice and idolatry. This is important for the church in a global age because globalism shows how connected our economies and governments can be. What affects people in other parts of the world affects us. Because of this, we have a responsibility to be good neighbors to people in other parts of the world.

Too many prosperity teachers turn a blind eye to the workings of capitalism among the poor. For example, during the time the prosperity message was growing in prominence in America "manufacturers were relocating from northern countries to the poor southern countries in search of the most vulnerable and desperate workers."[10] Major corporations like GE and IBM laid off large numbers of US workers and sent those jobs to poorer countries with less stringent labor laws and lower wages. The jobs went south but the goods came north. This was all done to exploit others and maximize profits.

---

8. Holliday, "Number of Billionaires Doubles Since Financial Crisis."

9. See also Monaghan, "US Wealth Inequality—top 0.1% worth as much as the bottom 90%."

10. Gallagher, *The True Cost of Low Prices*, 17.

- 83 percent of all clothing purchased in the US is made in poor countries
- 95 percent of shoes, sneakers, sporting goods, and computers are made in poor countries ($170 billion worth each year)
- 80 percent of toys are made in China ($29.4 billion worth each year)
- 100 percent of all televisions sold in the United States are produced in poor countries
- 80 percent of all electronics are made in poor countries[11]

Prosperity teachers did not say anything about this. They were encouraging people to get these products as signs of prosperity instead of speaking out on the unjust ways companies were exploiting people in other countries. There should be more to prosperity than consumption of goods. How goods are being produced and who is profiting from this are important matters. This is exactly why prosperity doctrine should not be the new Pentecostal message. Advocates of prosperity cannot continue to turn a blind eye to the inequitable workings of global capitalism and the idolatry of the market that exploits the many and profits the few.

CONCLUSION: PROSPERITY AS SHARED WEALTH AND BLESSING

Since the late fifties prosperity teachers have dealt with the issue of poverty because they had to convince many Pentecostals that God was good and wanted to bless them. Since the nineties, Pentecostals have become more accustomed to seeing wealthy and prosperous Christians. The culture of Pentecostalism has changed. Where does the prosperity movement go in order to possibly become the new Pentecostal message? I will provide one possibility for consideration. The next stage in the evolution of the prosperity message is teaching both prosperous believers in church and wealthy people in the world to share the wealth God placed on the earth. A. A. Allen, Oral Roberts, Ken Hagin, Kenneth and Gloria Copeland, Fred Price, Creflo Dollar, Jerry Savelle, Jesse Duplantis, and many others have attacked poverty in the church to show that God is not against wealthy and blessed people. These teachers have missed something, and what they've missed is the importance of shared blessing.

Poverty is really not the problem and it should not be the sole focus of prosperity teaching going forward. The problem is a failure to share

11. Ibid., 20.

wealth. Hinson-Hasty concludes, "Sacred stories, ancient traditions, and confessions of faith emphasize that when it comes to the wealth divide and poverty, the problem is wealth, not poverty."[12] Two examples of this can be found in the writings of the New Testament. First, the Gospel of Luke gives multiple warnings against the rich. "But woe to you who are rich, for you have already received your comfort" or "Watch out! Be on your guard against all kinds of greed; life does not consist in an abundance of possessions" (6:24; 12:15). Second, consider the deutero-Pauline text of 1 Timothy 6:9–10 that says, "Those who want to get rich fall into temptation and a trap and into many foolish and harmful desires that plunge people into ruin and destruction. For the love of money is a root of all kinds of evil. Some people, eager for money, have wandered from the faith, and pierced themselves with many griefs." While both texts warn the rich, the deeper issues they address are the liabilities of wealth. Such ancient texts lend credence to Hinson-Hasty's argument that the problem the ancient traditions spoke to was wealth, not poverty.

Early Christians recognized what is a glaring oversight for the church today. The problem is not the poor but the wealthy. Now the next generation of prosperity teachers need to turn their attention to the wealthy. Pentecostal prosperity teachers need to join theologians like Hinson-Hasty in addressing issues of global poverty and wealth. Doing this can restore the prophetic edge the movement had during the days of the Azusa Street Revival when blacks and whites worshiped together, going against the practice of racial segregation. Prosperity teaching can become a message about sharing God's wealth with all creation and rebuking the social tendency of the few who are rich to hoard wealth for themselves. This more mature form of prosperity teaching could do much good in a world of injustice and inequity.

Ironically, John Avanzini provides an opening to explore a message of shared blessing and wealth for all as God's intent in his book *The Wealth of the World*.[13] Earlier I mentioned Avanzini, a prominent prosperity teacher in the nineties, but I want to revisit his argument because it is particularly germane to the issue of wealth inequality. In his book, he argues that God placed enough wealth on the earth for everyone to be prosperous. He examines the wealth produced off natural resources and shows that trillions of dollars of wealth are produced from a few natural

---

12. Ibid., 50.
13. Avanzini, *The Wealth of the World*, 57–58.

resources. Avanzini makes a compelling argument but does not attempt to probe the deeper reasons as to why this wealth is not shared. Instead he wants to argue for a doctrine of prosperity beginning with divine intent for human flourishing. His work illustrates both the peril and promise of prosperity teaching. He should have addressed the disconnect between the wealth available from and for all creation *and* the abject poverty that is widespread in the world. But his work is also promising because he lays the groundwork for a theology of shared wealth.

If there is an abundance of wealth in various resources then it begs the question of why this wealth is not shared. So I ask, why aren't more advocates of prosperity who are prospering off the message they preach speaking out on the issue of the wealth inequality? This is what is missing in prosperity teaching. Instead of blaming the poor for their sin or lack of faith, teachers need to turn their attention to the wealthy and their preoccupation with profit and amassing the wealth of creation that should belongs to everyone. Whether teachers of prosperity, today and in the coming years, articulate the message of prosperity in these broader and more holistic terms will remain to be seen. The possibility is there for amended forms of prosperity teaching to revitalize global Pentecostalism. But to do so would require an understanding of the Spirit's work that is holistic. The outpouring of the Spirit manifests faith and dynamism inside the walls of the church and justice in the streets. I hope and pray that all God's children truly experience this kind of prosperity.

— Appendix —

Critiques of Prosperity Theology

Religious Scholar/ Popular Pastor	Publication	Critique(s)
Harold Wilmington	"Prosperity Theology: A Slot Machine Religion" (1987)	Prosperity theology is self-seeking and self-centered at its core. The belief in universal and immutable laws that govern all aspects of life is flawed and unbiblical. Believers are not little gods as Kenneth Copeland teaches. Misinterpretations of biblical texts like Joshua 1:8, Mark 10:29–30, Luke 6:38, and 3 John 2.
David Jones	"The Bankruptcy of the Prosperity Gospel" (1998)	Major errors in their understanding of the Abrahamic covenant; the atonement, giving, and faith. Misinterpretations of biblical texts like 3 John 2.
David T. Williams	"The Heresy of Prosperity Teaching" (1987)	Proofs of heretical nature of this movement are the "casualties of the faith message," which refer to those who give monies to Word of Faith ministries but do not receive promised blessings. Non-prosperity-teaching churches are left to deal with these people who are devastated by not experiencing prosperity they were promised. This teaching has defective views of both God and faith, especially the idea that positive confession forces God to act for the believer. This belief resembles pagan magic instead of the Bible.

David T. Williams	"Prosperity Teaching and Positive Thinking" (1987)	The origins of prosperity theology lay in New Thought metaphysics and Christian Science. The emphasis on positive thinking does not come from the Bible but from Norman Vincent Peale.
Dennis Hollinger	"Enjoying God Forever: A Historical and Sociological Profile of the Health and Wealth Gospel" (1997)	Uses the deprivation theory to explain why some people are drawn to the prosperity movement. People join religious sects to redress social needs. American cultural themes such as physical well-being, individualism, and personal financial success are behind the movement's growth.
Ken Sarles	"A Theological Evaluation of the Prosperity Gospel" (1986)	Prosperity theology is deeply flawed in its approach to biblical interpretation. Teachers proof text and rely on a flat literalism that misconstrues the meaning of biblical texts. Prosperity teachers begin with the American middle class experience and then baptize a handful of verses that seems to substantiate that experience.
John MacArthur	*Charismatic Chaos* (1992)	The prosperity movement is a false religion because it creates a god whose function is to deliver cargo to its adherents. It is a form of voodoo where God can be manipulated or controlled for human benefit.
Andrew Perriman	*Faith, Health, and Prosperity* (2003)	The belief in prosperity operates as a hermeneutical control that predetermines the way Scripture is read and guarantees the interpretive outcome. The belief in revelation knowledge affects how Scripture is interpreted as well.
Jeremiah Wright	*Blow the Trumpet in Zion* (2005)	Two mistakes that prosperity teachers make are equating capitalism with Christianity and neglecting the history of slavery and its influence on African Americans.

Author	Work	Critique
Robert Franklin	*Crisis in the Village* (2007)	The movement's teachers tend to focus on institutional well-being at the expense of serving the vulnerable. They deliberately suppress language about radical sacrifice for the sake of the kingdom. These teachers operate as spiritual entrepreneurs who produce and package user-friendly spirituality to large groups of people.
Milmon F. Harrison	*Righteous Riches: The Word of Faith Movement in Contemporary African American Religion* (2005)	The prosperity movement is not the first movement of this kind in the black community. Religious leaders like Rev. Ike, Johnnie Coleman, and Daddy Grace sought to meet spiritual and material needs of African Americans. This movement resonates with people who desire to be successful and is a type of a poor people's movement. It rests on the belief that America is a meritocracy and teachers do not seek to overthrow an unjust economic system but tell people to prosper within it.
D. R. McConnell	*A Different Gospel* (1995)	The roots of Word of Faith teaching go back to E. W. Kenyon and his reliance on New Thought metaphysic teachers like Mary Baker Eddy and Charles Emerson. There are also many theological and biblical errors, like the belief that believers are "king's kids."
Rob Starner	"Prosperity Theology" (2006)	Prosperity teachers wrongly insist that blessings are only material. Teachers lack biblical balance for a broader understanding of a good God.
Gordon Fee	*The Disease of the Health and Wealth Gospels* (1985)	Prosperity teaching is more a product of American society than the teachings of Scripture. The basic problem with this movement is its interpretation of the Bible. The belief that God's will for people to prosper financially controls how Scripture is read. Selectively read texts, which is an arbitrary and subjective way to interpret Scripture.

Author	Work	Summary
Deji Isaac Ayegboyin	"A Rethinking of Prosperity Teaching in the New Pentecostal Churches in Nigeria" (2006)	Prosperity teaching in Nigeria views God differently than older Pentecostals. For example, they believe that the name Jehovah Jireh implies that God is a God of abundance and God wants Christians to enjoy spiritual and material wealth. Other problems abound, such as teachers operating ministries as private businesses, the practice of giving money to the preacher to win God's favor, and the promise of the hundredfold return.
Peter Young	"Prosperity Teaching in an African Context" (1996)	A common belief in Africa is that Jesus came to establish the kingdom of God on earth. Because of this, teachers rarely mention the eschaton. All the benefits of the kingdom are available now. Another problematic belief is the tendency of teachers to attribute pain or poverty to some sin or defect in the spiritual life of the individual.
Young Hoon Lee	"The Case for Prosperity Theology" (1996)	The American expression of prosperity teaching is primarily self-centered.
James Hednut-Beumler	*In Pursuit of the Almighty's Dollar* (2007)	Prosperity teachers practice a form of magic with the belief that God can be manipulated for human benefit.
Stephanie Mitchem	*Name It and Claim It: Prosperity Preaching in the Black Church* (2007)	Prosperity preaching ties Christianity itself to the accumulation of wealth—the use of religion for gain. Religion becomes a tool for self-gratification and self-righteousness. Prosperity religions generally develop a theology of the here and now. The leaders do not draw from centuries of theological development but their decades of experience. Faith cannot be reduced to simple platitudes, even if they are taken from biblical passages.
Debra Mumford	*Exploring Prosperity Preaching* (2012)	Faith, hope, personal accountability, and the empowering work of the Holy Spirit are important and constructive teachings. But the major error of prosperity teachers is that they present faith, hope, accountability, and the Spirit as means to becoming rich.

Bibliography

Anderson, Allan. *African Reformation*. Trenton, NJ: Africa World, 2001.

———. *An Introduction to Pentecostalism*. New York: Cambridge University Press, 2004.

Anderson, C. Thomas. *How to Become a Millionaire God's Way*. New York: Faith Words, 2004.

Anderson, Robert Mapes. *Vision of the Disinherited*. New York: Oxford University Press, 1979.

Allen, A. A. *God's Guarantee to Prosper and Bless You Financially*. Miracle Valley, AZ: A. A. Allen Revivals, 1968.

———. *The Secret to Scriptural Financial Success*. Dallas: A. A. Allen Revivals, 1953.

———. *Self Invited Troubles*. Miracle Valley, AZ: A. A. Allen Revivals, 1965.

———. *Send Now Prosperity*. Miracle Valley, AZ: A. A. Allen Revivals, 1968.

———. *Your Christian Dollar*. Miracle Valley, AZ: A. A. Allen Revivals, 1958.

Avanzini, John. *Have a Good Report*. Tulsa: Harrison, 1991.

———. *John Avanzini Answers Your Questions about Biblical Economics*. Tulsa, OK: Harrison, 1992.

———. *Moving the Hand of God*. Tulsa, OK: Harrison, 1990.

———. *Rich God Poor God*. Tulsa, OK: Abel, 2001.

———. *War on Debt*. Tulsa, OK: Harrison, 1990.

———. *The Wealth of the World: The Proven Wealth Transfer System*. Tulsa, OK: Harrison, 1989.

Ayegboyin, Deji Isaac. "A Rethinking of Prosperity Teaching in the New Pentecostal Churches in Nigeria." *Black Theology* 4.1 (2006) 70–86.

Bakker, Jim. *Eight Keys to Success*. Charlotte, NC: Heritage Village Church and Missionary Fellowship, 1980.

———. *I Was Wrong*. Nashville: Thomas Nelson, 1997.

———. *Prosperity and the Coming Apocalypse*. Nashville: Thomas Nelson, 1998.

———. *Showers of Blessings*. Charlotte, NC: Heritage Village Church and Missionary Fellowship, 1986.

Barron, Bruce. *The Health and Wealth Gospel*. Downers Grove, IL: InterVarsity, 1987.

Bartleman, Frank. *Azusa Street: How Pentecost Came to Los Angeles*. Gainesville, FL: Bridge-Logos, 1980.

Beumler, James Hednut. *In Pursuit of the Almighty's Dollar: A History of Money in American Protestantism*. Chapel Hill, NC: University of North Carolina Press, 2007.

Biema, David Van, and Jeff Chu. "Does God Want You to be Rich?" *Time* (September 18, 2006) 48–56.

Blomberg, Craig. *Neither Poverty Nor Riches: A Biblical Theology of Possessions.* Downers Grove, IL: InterVarsity, 2001.

Bowers, James Philemon. *You Can Have What You Say: A Pastoral Response to the Prosperity Gospel.* Cleveland, TN: Center for Pentecostal Leadership and Care, 2004.

Bowler, Kate. *Blessed: A History of the American Prosperity Gospel.* New York: Oxford University Press, 2013.

Bowman, Robert M. *The Word-Faith Controversy.* Grand Rapids: Baker, 2001.

Burgess, Stanley, ed. *Encyclopedia of Pentecostal and Charismatic Christianity.* New York: Routledge, 2006.

———. *New International Dictionary of the Pentecostal Charismatic Movement.* Grand Rapids: Zondervan, 2003.

Byassee, Jason. "The Health and Wealth Gospel: Be Happy." *Christian Century* 122.14 (2007) 20–23.

Caldwell, Kirbyjon. *Entrepreneurial Faith.* Colorado Springs: Waterbrook, 2004.

Carruthers, Iva E., Frederick Haynes III, and Jeremiah Wright. *Blow the Trumpet in Zion: Global Vision and Action for the 21st Century Black Church.* Minneapolis: Fortress, 2005.

Cho, Paul Yonggi. *Salvation, Health, and Prosperity: Our Threefold Blessings in Christ.* 1990.

Copeland, Kenneth. "Delight in the Good Life." *Believers Voice of Victory* (May 2007) 4–7.

———. "Heirs of the World." *Believers Voice of Victory* (August 2007) 4–8.

———. *The Laws of Prosperity.* Fort Worth, TX: Kenneth Copeland Ministries, 1995.

———. "Live in the Blessing." *Believer's Voice of Victory* (September 2007) 4–8.

———. *Prosperity: The Choice is Yours.* Forth Worth, TX: Kenneth Copeland Ministries, 1985.

Copeland, Gloria. *God's Will Is Prosperity.* Fort Worth: Kenneth Copeland, 1978.

Council of Economic Advisors for the President's Initiative on Race. *Changing America: Indicators of Social and Economic Well-Being by Race and Hispanic Origin.* Washington, DC: U. S. Government Printing Office, 1998.

Dayton, Donald. *Theological Roots of Pentecostalism.* Grand Rapids: Eerdmans, 1975.

DePriest, Tomika. "Economic Deliverance Thru The Church: Black Churches and Black Economic Development." *Black Enterprise* (February 1997), http://www.blackenterprise.com/mag/economic-deliverance-thru-the-church/6/.

Dollar, Creflo. *Claim Your Victory Today.* New York: Faith Words, 2006.

———. *No More Debt.* College Park, GA: Creflo Dollar Ministries, 2001.

———. *Total Life Prosperity.* Nashville: Thomas Nelson, 1999.

Faupel, William. *The Everlasting Gospel.* Sheffield, UK: Sheffield, 1996.

Fee, Gordon D. *The Disease of the Health and Wealth Gospels.* Beverly, MA: Frontline, 1985.

Ford, Clifford. "God's Real Estate Man." In *God's Formula for Success and Prosperity*, edited by Oral Roberts and G. H. Montgomery, 7–20. United States: America's Healing Magazine, 1955.

Franklin, Robert. *Another Day's Journey: Black Churches Confront the American Crisis.* Minneapolis: Fortress, 1997.

———. *Crisis in the Village: Restoring Hope in African American Communities.* Minneapolis: Fortress, 2007.
Gallagher, Vincent A. *The True Cost of Low Prices.* New York: Orbis, 2006.
Gasque, W. Ward. "Prosperity Theology and the New Testament." *Evangelical Review of Theology* 20.1 (1996) 40–48.
Garrison, Becky. "It's All About the Dough Re Me at Creflo's New York Show." *The Wittenburg Door* (July/August) 28–31.
Greer, Rowan A., ed. *Origen, An Exhortation to Martyrdom, Prayer and Selected Works.* Classics of Western Spirituality. New York: Paulist, 1979.
Gushee, David P. *Toward a Just and Caring Society: Christian Responses to Poverty in America.* Grand Rapids: Baker, 1999.
Hagin, Ken. *Bible Faith Study Course.* Tulsa, OK: Rhema Bible Church, 1991.
———. *Bible Prayer Study Course.* Tulsa, OK: Rhema Bible Church, 1991.
———. *Biblical Keys to Financial Prosperity.* Tulsa, OK: Rhema Bible Church, 1995.
———. *Don't Blame God.* Tulsa, OK: Rhema Bible Church, 1979.
———. *El Shaddai: The God Who Is More Than Enough.* Tulsa, OK: Faith Library, 1980.
———. *Godliness is Profitable.* Tulsa, OK: Rhema Bible Church, 1982.
———. *The Holy Spirit and His Gifts.* Tulsa, OK: Rhema Bible Church, 1991.
———. *How To Write Your Own Ticket With God.* Tulsa, OK: Rhema Bible Church, 1979.
———. *In Him.* Tulsa, OK: Rhema Bible Church, 1980.
———. *The Midas Touch.* Tulsa, OK: Rhema Bible Church, 2000.
———. *You Can Have What You Say.* Tulsa, OK: Rhema Bible Church, 1991.
Hannegraff, Hank. *Christianity in Crisis.* Eugene, OR: Harvest, 1997.
Harrison, Milmon F. *Righteous Riches: The Word of Faith Movement in Contemporary African American Religion.* New York: Oxford University Press, 2005.
Hinson-Hasty, Elizabeth. "The Problem of Wealth." *Cross Currents* (March 2014) 39–58.
Holliday, Katie. "Number of Billionaires Doubles Since Financial Crisis." *CNBC*, October 30, 2014, http://www.cnbc.com/id/102134929#.
Hollinger, Dennis. "Enjoying God Forever: A Historical/Sociological Profile of the Health and Wealth Gospel." In *The Gospel and Contemporary Perspectives*, edited by Douglas Moo, 13–26. Grand Rapids: Kregel, 1997.
Hunter, Bob. "Christianity Still in Crisis: A Word of Faith Update." *Christian Research Journal* 30.3 (2007) 12–33.
Jackson, Robert. "Prosperity Theology and the Faith Movement." *Themelios* 15 (1989) 16–24.
Jakes, T. D. *Can You Stand to be Blessed?* Shippensburg, PA: Treasure, 1994.
———. *The Great Investment: Faith, Family, and Finances.* New York: G. P. Putnam Sons, 2000.
———. *Maximize the Moment.* New York: Berkley, 1999.
———. *Reposition Yourself.* New York: Atria, 2007.
Jones, David W. "The Bankruptcy of the Prosperity Gospel: An Exercise in Biblical and Theological Ethics." *Faith and Mission* (Fall 1998) 79–87.
Jones, David W., and Russell S. Woodbridge. *Health, Wealth, and Happiness.* Grand Rapids: Kregel, 2011.
Kim, Sang Bok David. "A Bed of Roses or a Bed of Thorns." *Evangelical Review of Theology* 20.1 (1996) 14–25.

King, Robert. "Indianapolis Church Mixes Fiscal Spiritual Messages." *Louisville Courier Journal,* June 3, 2007.

Lee, Shayne. *T. D. Jakes: America's New Preacher.* New York: New York University Press, 2005.

Levs, Joshua. "African American Churches Weigh Gospel Debate." *NPR,* http://www.npr.org/templates/story/story.php?storyId=4779412.

———. "America's Black Churches Debate Role in Society." *VOA,* http://www.voanews.com/content/a-13-2005-08-17-voa22/302987.html.

Lincoln, C. Eric. *The Black Church in the African American Experience.* Durham, NC: Duke University Press, 1990.

Long, Eddie. *It's Your Time.* New Kensington, PA: Whitaker, 2007.

———. *Taking Over.* Lake Mary, FL: Charisma, 1999.

MacArthur, John. *Charismatic Chaos.* Grand Rapids: Zondervan, 1992.

Mackie, Alexander. *The Gift of Tongues: A Story of the Pathological Aspect of Christianity.* New York: George H. Doran, 1921.

McConnell, D. R. *A Different Gospel.* Peabody, MA: Hendrickson, 1995.

Miller, Donald E., and Tetsuano Yamamori. *Global Pentecostalism.* Berkeley, CA: University of California Press, 2007.

Mitchem, Stephanie Y. *Name it and Claim It: Prosperity Preaching in the Black Church.* Cleveland: Pilgrim, 2007.

Monaghan, Angela. "US Wealth Inequality—top 0.1% worth as much as the bottom 90%." *The Guardian,* November 13, 2014, http://www.theguardian.com/business/2014/nov/13/us-wealth-inequality-top-01-worth-as-much-as-the-bottom-90.

Montgomery, Ed. *Breaking the Spirit of Poverty.* Lake Mary, FL: Charisma, 1998.

Moo, Douglas. *The Gospel and Contemporary Perspectives.* Grand Rapids: Kregel, 1997.

Mumford, Debra. *Exploring Prosperity Preaching.* Valley Forge, PA: Judson, 2012.

Murphy, Ed. *Handbook of Spiritual Warfare.* Nashville: Thomas Nelson, 1996.

Perriman, Andrew. *Faith, Health, and Prosperity.* Great Britain: Paternoster, 2003.

Phiri, Isaac, and Joe Maxwell. "Gospel Riches." *Christianity Today* 51.7 (2007) 22–29.

Pinn, Anthony. *The Black Church in the Post Civil Rights Era.* Maryknoll, NY: Orbis, 2009.

Price, Frederick K. C. *Answered Prayer Guaranteed.* Lake Mary, FL: Charisma, 2006.

———. *Higher Finance: How to Live Debt Free.* Los Angeles: Faith One, 1999.

———. *How Faith Works.* Los Angeles: Faith One, 2001.

———. *Is Healing for All?* Los Angeles: Faith One, 1976.

———. *Name It and Claim It: The Power of Positive Confession.* Los Angeles: Faith One, 1992.

———. *Now Faith Is Substance Evidence Hebrews 11:1.* Los Angeles: Faith One, 1998.

———. *The Purpose of Prosperity.* Los Angeles: Faith One, 2001.

———. *Race, Religion and Racism.* Vol. 1: *A Bold Encounter With the Division in the Church.* Los Angeles: Faith One, 1999.

———. *Race, Religion and Racism.* Vol. 2: *Perverting the Gospel to Subjugate a People.* Los Angeles: Faith One, 2001.

———. *Race, Religion and Racism.* Vol. 3: *Jesus, Christianity and Islam.* Los Angeles: Faith One, 2002.

Roberts, Oral. *Attack Your Lack.* Tulsa, OK: Oral Roberts, 1985.

———. *Flood Stage: Opening the Windows of Heaven.* Tulsa, OK: Oral Roberts, 1981.

———. *God Is a Good God: Believe It and Come Alive.* Indianapolis: Bobbs-Merrill, 1960.

———. *God's Formula for Success and Prosperity.* Tulsa, OK: Healing Waters, 1955.

———. *Miracle of Seed Faith.* Tulsa, OK: Oral Roberts, 1970.

———. *My Story.* Tulsa, OK: privately published, 1961.

Sanders, Ellen. "The Greatest Threat to the Black Church." *Gospel Today* (May-June 2007) 26–31.

Sarles, Ken. "A Theological Evaluation of the Prosperity Gospel." *Bibliotheca Sacra* (October/December 1986) 329–52.

Savelle, Jerry. *Prosperity of the Soul.* Tulsa, OK: Harrison, 1979.

Schaull, Richard, and Waldo Cesar. *Pentecostalism and the Future of the Christian Churches.* Grand Rapids: Eerdmans, 2000.

Schneider, John R. *The Good of Affluence: Seeking God in a Culture of Wealth.* Grand Rapids: Eerdmans, 2002.

Schuller, Robert. *The Be Happy Attitudes: Eight Positive Attitudes that Can Transform Your Life.* Dallas: Word, 1996.

Simmons, Martha. "Trends in the African American Church." *African American Pulpit* 10.2 (2007) 9–16.

Starner, Rob. "Prosperity Theology." In *Encyclopedia of Pentecostal and Charismatic Christianity*, edited by Stanley Burgess. New York: Routledge, 2006.

"State and County Quickfacts." *U.S. Census Bureau*, December 4, 2014, http://quickfacts.census.gov/qfd/states/54000.html.

Synan, Vinson. *An Eyewitness Remembers the Century of the Holy Spirit.* Grand Rapids: Chosen, 2010.

———. *Holiness-Pentecostal Tradition.* Grand Rapids: Eerdmans, 1997.

———. *In The Latter Days.* N.p.: Xulon, 2001.

———. Interview on Prosperity Gospel. Regent University, October 11, 2006.

"Ten Most Depressing States in the U.S." *Health.com*, http://www.health.com/health/gallery/0,,20483493_11,00.html.

Thomas, Stacey-Floyd, et al. *Black Church Studies: An Introduction.* Nashville: Abingdon, 2007.

Thompson, Leroy. *I'll Never Be Broke.* Darrow, LA: Ever Increasing Ministries, 2001.

———. *Money Cometh to the Body of Christ.* Tulsa, OK: Harrison, 1999.

———. *Money Thou Art Loosed.* Darrow, LA: Ever Increasing Ministries, 2001.

Trull, Joe. *Walking in the Way: An Introduction to Christian Ethics.* Nashville: Broadman and Holman, 1997.

Tuchman, Gary. "What Is a Christian?" *Anderson Cooper 360 Degrees* (May 11, 2007).

Wacker, Grant. *Heaven Below: Early Pentecostals and American Culture.* Cambridge, MA: Harvard University Press, 2001.

Walker, Hezekiah. *Destiny: Dream It Declare It Do It.* New Kensington, PA: Whitaker, 2003.

Weeks, Thomas. *Even as Your Soul Prospers.* Tulsa, OK: Harrison, 2004.

"West Virginia Vital Statistics Summary." *Health Statistics Center for the West Virginia Department of Health and Human Resources*, December 2, 2014, http://www.wvdhhr.org/bph/hsc/Statserv/Stat_Triv.asp.

Wheeler, Sondra Ely. *Wealth as Peril and Obligation: The New Testament on Possessions.* Grand Rapids: Eerdmans, 1995.

Williams, David T. "The Heresy of Prosperity Teaching." *Journal of South African Theology* 61.1 (December 1987) 33–44.

———. "Prosperity Teaching and Positive Thinking." *Evangelical Review of Theology* 11.4 (October 1987) 197–208.

Wilmington, Harold L. "Prosperity Theology: A Slot Machine Religion." *Fundamentalist Journal* 6.10 (1987) 15–18.

Winter, Ralph, and Steven Hawthorne. *Perspectives on World Christian Movement*. Pasadena, CA: William Carey Library, 1999.

Yong, Amos. *The Spirit Poured Out on All Flesh: Pentecostalism and the Possibility of Global Pentecostal Theology*. Grand Rapids: Baker, 2005.

Young-Hoon, Lee. "The Case for Prosperity Theology." *Evangelical Review of Theology* 20.1 (1996) 26–39.

Young, Peter R. "Prosperity Teaching in an African Context." *African Journal of Evangelical Theology* 15.1 (1996) 3–18.

www.ingramcontent.com/pod-product-compliance
Lightning Source LLC
Chambersburg PA
CBHW030903170426
43193CB00009BA/723